Within
Sebastopol

CAPTAIN CHODASIEWICZ (HODASEVICH)

Within Sebastopol

A Narrative of the Campaign in the
Crimea, and of the Events of the Siege

K. Hodasevich,

LEONAUR

Within Sebastopol
K. Hodasevich,

First published under the title
A Voice From Within
the Walls of Sebastopol:
1856

Leonaur is an imprint
of Oakpast Ltd

Copyright in this form © 2008 Oakpast Ltd

ISBN: 978-1-84677-572-7 (hardcover)
ISBN: 978-1-84677-571-0 (softcover)

http://www.leonaur.com

Publisher's Notes

In the interests of authenticity, the spellings, grammar and place names
used have been retained from the original editions.

The opinions of the authors represent a view of events in which he
was a participant related from his own perspective,
as such the text is relevant as an historical document.

The views expressed in this book are not necessarily
those of the publisher.

Contents

Preface

The present work, written by a Pole who served long in the Russian army, is chiefly based on notes and memoranda made during his period of service, and its publication is due to the urgent representations of several English gentlemen who became acquainted with the author in the Crimea. In addition to the new and interesting information given in the work, it affords important proof of the fallacy of the reports so diligently spread by certain parties, that the Polish nationality if destroyed, and that, save in the hearts of a few scattered exiles, the distinction between Russian and Pole has been obliterated. The career of the writer of this work gives a triumphant *démenti* to this assertion, so often indignantly repudiated by the Poles, and the more so as he hears testimony to the fact that the greater number of his countrymen serving in the ranks of the Russian army is animated by the same feelings as himself.

Captain Hodasevich [1] was only nine years of age when, by request, which in the Russian meaning of the word signifies the same as by order, he was sent to the Military Academy in St. Petersburg, and educated for the profession of arms. Though not allowed during his stay at the academy to speak or to read the Polish language, he not only did not forget his native tongue, but cherished in his bosom that spirit of Polish patriotism which the protracted misfortunes of the country, instead of deadening,

---

1. The correct spelling of the name is "Chodasiewicz;" but it is printed as "Hodasevich" in order to render the pronunciation of it less difficult to Englishmen, and as the name by which the author has been generally known whilst on the British Staff in the Crimea.

as is maintained by some, on the contrary tend to keep alive in the heart of the nation. Being employed during the late war in the army opposed to the French and English in the Crimea, and having heard a rumour of the intended formation of a Polish legion to act against Russia, Captain Hodasevich seized the first favourable opportunity to pass over to the Allies with a countryman of his, Mr. Römer, both being actuated by the hope of attaining a position in which they would be able to serve their country—a hope which would have led to a far greater number of desertions among the Poles than actually took place, had any encouragement been given by the Allies. Employed on the British Staff, our author furnished the military authorities with the most valuable information and excellent plans relative to the state and the position of the Russian forces, and it is but just to add that his services were duly appreciated.

The name of Captain Hodasevich is thus honourably associated with the names of the various other Poles who have rendered eminent services to the Allies in the late war, such as Iskander Bey, now Iskander Pasha (Ilinski), whose exploits in the army of Omar Pasha are so well known; as Hidaiot, who, serving in the same corps, and acting as interpreter to Captain Dymock at the passage of the Ingour, induced the Russian soldiers to fly, leaving their artillery on the ground, by addressing them in their own language with admirable presence of mind, and telling them that they were surrounded; as Sadyk Pasha (Czaykowski), who, with his regiment of Cossacks, fought so bravely on the Danube; as Colonel Kuczynski, chief of the staff of the Egyptian army at Eupatoria, who was ever foremost in the ranks against the Russians; as Majors Kleczynski and Jerzmanowski, who distinguished themselves in the Turkish army; and, lastly, as General Count Zamoyski, commanding the division of Cossacks of the Sultan, composed exclusively of Poles, among the number of whom there are many who had deserted from the Russian army, thus giving proof of the strong vitality of the Polish nationality, and of that unrelenting hatred of the people against the Russians, which, according to Captain Hodasevich, was so strongly manifested during the war, that severe measures were taken to repress it, and that the Russians used invariably to attribute their defeats to the agency of the Poles serving in the army, while the latter themselves, far from, attaching any idea of disgrace to desertion from the Russian ranks, looked upon their escape from the hated yoke as nothing more than a continuation of that emigration which will never cease as long as the tyranny which now oppresses Poland continues to weigh upon the country.

The Editor.

June, 1856.

Chapter 1

Into Sebastopol

The first and second battalions of the regiment of Chasseurs Taroutine, of the Second brigade of the 17th division of the Sixth corps of Infantry, reached Simpheropol on the 22nd of April, 1854. Through the interest of Major-General Volkhoff, the colonel of our regiment, we remained two days in this town.

Simpheropol, the chief town of the government of Tauride, is regularly built. In it, as usual in Russian towns, the Government buildings occupy the first place. The part in which the Tatars live is neither very clean nor very regular. In front of the cathedral is the monument to the memory of Dalgorouky Krimsky, conqueror of the Crimea.

On Easter Sunday (23rd of April) there was a religious service on the boulevard, conducted with all the pomp of the Greek Church, at which the men of our battalions were present. After this they received, each man, two large glasses of vodka (corn-brandy), a piece of white bread, and a pound and a half of beef; the whole of this feast being presented by the inhabitants of the town. It is a question not very difficult to answer whether this was voluntarily given, or simply that the orders of the Governor, Major-General Pestal, were obeyed in this respect: I can only state that more than one passed the night at the police station because he could or would not contribute his share towards the feast for the soldiers.

Nor were the police officers without their own profits upon

this occasion, for they seldom miss an opportunity like the present of improving the state of their funds. The people groan under the weight of the taxes, while the Governor raises contributions, for which he alone receives the reward in the shape of a cross or star, as the commanders of regiments report all these events to the Minister of War.

In the evening the band and chorus [1] of our regiment were on the boulevard, where they played and sang to the delight of the inhabitants, who had, *nolens volens,* so liberally contributed the soldiers' dinner on this day. Next evening I called upon Lieutenant Stepanoff, who had risen from the ranks, to persuade him to accompany me to the ball given that night in the assembly rooms. To all my arguments he answered, "What shall I do there? There will be a crowd of great folks there as well as our colonel; I cannot dance, so what can I do there? Besides, I shall be obliged to wear my uniform, and buy a pair of gloves. You had better not go: I bought today some capital brandy, so you had better remain with me, and we will amuse ourselves with something really useful and agreeable! Let those who like it jump and skip about like madmen; we at least will prove that we possess common sense."

These were the words of an officer of the line who had risen from the ranks, in which he had served twelve years; during which time he had practically an opportunity of judging of the efficiency of physical punishments upon his own person. Such men are esteemed good officers, because ready to fulfil all the commands of their colonel, even to dishonouring themselves, without using their own powers of reasoning. They are generally men of experience, and know how to acquire and take care of a kopeck for a rainy day, no matter how acquired. They form a miserable, though, unfortunately, a numerous class in the Russian army, where promotion from the ranks is on a large scale, as no means are taken to encourage the enlistment of respectable persons. I was heartily tired of attempting to persuade them out

---

1. In every Russian regiment a number of the men who possess good voices form a chorus; they sing military and other songs.

of their foolish and unfounded ideas.

Leaving this brother officer, I returned to my quarters, where I had a long conversation with the landlord about the present war.

"How unjust," said he, "it is of the English and French to interfere in this war! What had they to do with our quarrels? The war with Turkey is about the oppression of the Christians in the East, our brethren in faith; who will interfere for them if we do not? Besides, it is mentioned in the *Revelations* that the city of Byzantium is to be taken by Constantine;—our Emperor Nicholas has a son Constantine, who will go with his fleet and conquer Constantinople."

I believe the ship *Constantine* was built for the purpose of carrying the future conqueror to the scene of his glory; she was, however, never properly finished, as the Emperor had named a particular day on which he intended to inspect this vessel, and she was launched in a hurry to be ready by the appointed time, and consequently incomplete. Thus in a despotic country are the best schemes defeated.

Previously to this conversation I always had a good opinion of the understanding of my host, as he was one of the *chinovnicks* of the government offices. I did not contradict him, but tried to agree with him, out of respect to his grey hairs, and not to have in him an enemy; but what kept me from speaking my mind freely was the fact that I wore the uniform of a Russian officer in a time of war. I was ever very careful on similar occasions, as more than once I have been asked to tell my religion; on my replying "Catholic," "That's enough," would be the universal exclamation; "he is a Pole; you will never be able to convince him; he always wishes evil to our cause."

On the 25th April, at 5 a.m., I left Simpheropol with my company for Bakchi Sarai, which town we did not reach till late in the evening, after a harassing march.

Bakchi Sarai is, as it were, in a basin, being surrounded on every side by high mountains. The inhabitants are chiefly Tatars, who live in houses built after the Oriental fashion, of one story, within courtyards that open upon narrow, dirty streets. The most remarkable building in the town is the palace of the ancient *khans*, which, since the opening of the war, has been used as a military hospital. This is the scene of one of the Russian poet Pushkine's most beautiful poems, "The Fountain of Bachchi Sarai."

The Tatars here, and at other places in the Crimea, did not receive us *aux bras ouverts*; on the contrary, they appeared to look upon us with anything but friendly eyes. During our march through Russia, the soldiers were invariably fed by the generosity, forced or voluntary, of the different towns and villages on the road; but in the Crimea we were obliged to depend upon our rations and such other means as we might have at our disposal, the same as in an enemy's country.

The next day we left for the town of Sevastopol, which we reached after two days' march, which ended our long and fatiguing journey from Nijni Novgorod, whence we started six months before. On our arrival, the regiment to which I belonged occupied the barracks of Alexander on the Karabelnaya. The weather was wretched and the mud fearful; in consequence I remained cooped up in my quarters a whole week, and got fairly rested after my long and dreary march. Upon the arrival of fine weather I sallied forth to view the town and fortifications, since so celebrated. I remarked, among other things, the preponderance of public edifices, the chief of which were the Assembly Rooms, the Naval Library, the Theatre, the Governor's house, and some other buildings. The Greek and Catholic churches are well built (the former standing on a hill behind the Flagstaff battery). The house in which Prince Menschikoff lived is called the Palace of Katherine, and consists of a small building of one story opposite the wharf called Grafsky, near the battery of St. Nicholas.

Of the fortifications, the appearance of Fort St. Nicholas from the sea is very formidable—but the appearance alone is formidable, as two hundred shots fired at it would bring it about the ears of its defenders; the materials used in its construction being of a very inferior quality: no doubt the engineer who was charged with this work made good the deficiency by well fortifying his own pocket, according to the custom of such gentry in Russia.

On the other side of Artillery Bay (which, by the by, is called Artillery Bay because here is the arsenal of Sevastopol) there was an open earthwork called Battery 8: it was armed with twenty heavy guns, From this battery begins the stone wall that was to have surrounded the town, but was discontinued early in the year 1854 in consequence of an observation made by a colonel of the Engineers of the Guard, that it would impede the extension of the town. The expense of this work may also have had its influence; it was never carried beyond the tower in front of the barracks. This wall was about nine feet high and three feet thick, and in some places there were two guns planted for the purpose of enfilading the dead space along the line of defence. In this wall was built a corn magazine, and a little beyond at the end of the wall was a small tower, in which, at the time I first saw it, there were no guns mounted.

At the end of the boulevard there were the remains of an old work, which could only be traced by the half-filled-up ditch and the trodden-down breastwork.

In the Alexander battery there were fifteen guns; this work was built of stone, but was very old and much dilapidated.

The battery No. 10, near Quarantine Bay, was entirely open towards the south; not more than thirty guns were mounted in it.

On the right-hand side of the southern harbour there only existed Fort St. Paul, of which the engineer was a conscientious man, so that the walls were formed of enormous blocks of stone, put together with good lime cement.

On the north side, or Severnaya, is Fort Constantine, built in the same manner as Fort Nicholas, except that the upper line of guns is open. The battery of St. Michael is better built, except that the arches are rather thin, but not to any great extent. Fort Severnaya is useless, or worse than useless, as it is not properly commanded by other works, but by the high ground around it, so that at a distance of a grape-shot it is possible to see all the interior, even the barbette of the guns. Major-General Pavlovsky, who had charge of the fortifications of Sevastopol, proposed to destroy the North Fort as perfectly useless, as it was impossible to increase the wall, because the buildings (hospital, barracks, &c.) inside the fort were too near the wall. The citadel of the fort was in a state of neglect; not a single gun was mounted; the only thing remarkable was a subterranean passage from the citadel to the Soukhaya Balka. The length of this passage is about 4000 feet. In the whole North Fort there were not more than eight guns, and these in a very dilapidated state.

This was the state of the fortifications of Sevastopol at the time of which I write. But in the arsenal I remarked a large store of guns of different calibres, but very few mortars or gun-carriages. There were large stores of timber at the Admiralty Wharf and at the end of Artillery Bay.

I was incited by curiosity to ascertain the cause of the enormous stores of guns at Sevastopol, and learnt that Sevastopol was the storehouse for the Crimea and the forts of the eastern coast of the Black Sea, and consequently all the old guns from the Caucasus were sent to Sevastopol, as well as those from the different places in the Crimea. The guns that could be repaired were returned to the forts to which they belonged after the necessary reparation, while those which were worn out were put into store. Another reason for the number of guns in this town was, that the ships of the Black Sea fleet were built and armed at Nicholayeff, whence they were brought to Sevastopol; and when they were broken up in the latter place, their guns were placed in store. The consequence is, that during a period of seventy years the number of guns has increased to something enormous. The number of convicts confined in the town amounted to about seven thousand men, whom Menschikoff employed upon the fortifications of the harbour.

According to orders I received, I took up my quarters with my company in Fort St. Nicholas, where I remained till we took the field.

The following are the troops that occupied the Crimea in the month of May, 1854:—2nd (Chasseur) brigade of the 17th division of Infantry, consisting of the regiments of Borodino, being that of His Imperial Highness the Hereditary Grand Duke, and Taroutine, to which I belonged; the number of men in this brigade was about 5500, under the command of the General of division, Lieutenant-General Kiriakoff. Attached to our brigade were the 4th and 5th Light Field batteries of the 17th brigade of Artillery.[2]

It was originally intended that we should go to the Caucasus, or, as some said, to India; for this reason the 3rd division, consisting of four guns from each battery of the 17th and 18th divisions, were ordered to be sent to Sevastopol as a reserve of artillery for the army of the Caucasus. From the town of Bachmout, in the government of Ekaterinoslav, our march was changed: the 1st brigade of our division going to the Caucasus, where it occupied Taman, Anapa, and Novorossisk, on the eastern shore of the Black Sea; while our 2nd brigade moved towards Sevastopol: consequently in each of our batteries there only remained eight guns instead of twelve, which is the war complement.

Besides our brigade, there were in the Crimea four reserve and four depot battalions of the 13th division under the command of Major-General Oslonovich; the number of men in these battalions was about 7000 (the 13th division of the active army was transported across the Black Sea to Redout Kalé by the whole of the Russian fleet about the month of March, 1854); the 1st brigade of the 14th division, consisting of the regiments of Volhynia and Minsk, under the command of the general of division Major-General Von Moller, about 5000 men, with two field batteries of twelve guns each. Near Sevastopol was the 2nd brigade of the 6th division of Cavalry, consisting of two regiments of Hussars, under the command of Major-General Khaletzky, with one battery of horse artillery—their strength

---

2. To every division there is a brigade of artillery corresponding in number. Thus, the 17th division has the 17th brigade of Artillery.

amounted to about 1800 men; with one regiment of Cossacks of the Don. This will give 17,500 bayonets, 600 foot artillerymen, 2400 sabres, and 180 horse artillerymen. The number of sailors of the Black Sea fleet, including the different workmen belonging to the docks, would be about 25,000 men.

Up to the 27th of August the following additions had been made to the fortifications of the town:—The full number of guns had been placed in the lower tier of Fort St. Nicholas; in the second tier, guns had been placed in every second embrasure facing the entrance to the harbour; while on the side to the north, which is three stories high, the second tier had guns only in the third and sometimes fourth embrasures; in the third tier it was considered dangerous to place any guns, and consequently very few were placed there.

Every third gun was fired for practice, which shook the whole fort, and the embrasures were spoilt by the falling of a great many stones, so that the next day parties of workmen were ordered to repair the damage caused, and then I saw that the walls were only faced with stone, the space between which was filled up with rubbish. In the battery No. 8 a considerable number of guns were added, as well as a furnace for heating shot. A new façade was added to this battery, on the left-hand side, for the purpose of enfilading Fort Alexander. In this addition to the old work were placed twelve heavy guns; two large powder magazines were also constructed at this place, where a flag was constantly displayed during the siege.

Additions were also made to Fort Alexander for the purpose of enfilading the battery No. 10 . In the battery No. 10 a large number of guns were added, and in front of this battery, on the sea-shore, a palisade was erected in the form of a lunette, from which to the east and south the palisade was continued. In Quarantine Bay, near the quarantine buildings, there was placed in shallow water an old frigate fully armed. This frigate defended the entrance to Quarantine Bay. Forts St. Michael and St. Paul were armed with their full complements of guns. Fort Constantine had not the full number of guns in the lower tier.

The tower of Volkhoff was built in consequence of the following circumstance:—A steamer belonging to the allied fleet approached the town, and put down a buoy, which was afterwards remarked by Admiral Korniloff, who then discovered that this spot could not be reached by any of the grins of the forts, and consequently would have proved a safe position for the ships of the allied fleet from which to bombard the town. In consequence of this discovery a contractor was sought who would undertake to build a battery in such a position as to command this spot; a contractor appeared in the person of a merchant of Sevastopol, called Volkhoff, who engaged to construct the required battery at his own expense, and it cost him 8000 silver *roubles.*

Of course it was a matter of doubt whether M. Volkhoff went to this expense at his own wish or by order of the authorities; the necessary work was performed, and in Russia it is not always possible nor safe to try to find out by what means. The position of this tower is excellent, and commands a large extent; it is not more than twelve or fifteen yards from the sea, from which, however, it is hidden by a very high glacis, so that a ship within cannon-shot cannot see her enemy, though she can feel it. On the land side this tower is equally effective. It is two stories high, if that is a correct expression when the upper story is almost level with the surface. In the lower story are the powder and other magazines for the use of the garrison of this tower; there are in this story eight small carronades, and loopholes for small arms, which can only be used to defend the ditch and glacis. On the upper story, which is built on arches, there are eight heavy guns, which can be used in any direction, as they are capable of being turned on pivots in every way. There is a deep ditch to the very foundation, with a drawbridge on the south side. Between the tower and the sea there are two wells of excellent water. This tower was finished and consecrated in the month of June, 1854.

The North Fort, or Severnaya Oukreplenie, cost much trouble to be made useful. From the bottom of the ditch a stone wall was built a foot and a half in thickness at the top, which admitted an increase of thickness, and in consequence height, to the wall, so that it became impossible to see the interior of the fort. The width of the ditch was augmented to ten feet, with a stone scarp. In this fort there were few guns—towards the sea only four. The closed battery No. 4 was constructed of earth faced on the outside with flat pieces of stone; it contained twenty guns, all bearing upon the harbour. In Krim Balka lay an old dismasted frigate, with guns on one side only, and these turned towards the harbour.

Near the garden of Admiral Nakhimoff (Golandia) a battery was constructed mounting twelve guns, and on the opposite side of the harbour another battery of twelve guns. Across the harbour, from Fort St. Michael to Fort St, Nicholas, were placed two strong booms, with an entrance near Fort St, Michael. Four vessels were moored in the southern harbour, with the greater part of the steamers of the fleet. Two frigates were moored behind the booms, and eight ships were placed in two lines opposite Krim Balka, with their broadsides turned towards the entrance of the harbour. All the smaller merchant-vessels were sent up to the head of the harbour towards Inkerman.

From these arrangements it is evident that Prince Menschikoff expected his visitors from the sea, but that he never dreamt of their coming from the land side.

On the 13th of June, 1854, I left the town and encamped on the north side, where was the 2nd brigade of the 17th division, with the 4th and 5th light batteries of our brigade of artillery, and the 12th battery of horse artillery belonging to the 2nd brigade of the 6th division of cavalry, which was encamped on the river Katcha. Our camp was about two *versts* from the village of Ychkooevka, whence the Black Sea was seen spread as it were at our feet, and here I had the pleasure of my first sea-bath.

On the heights above the village we used to rush out of our tents when any straggler brought us intelligence that the enemy's vessels were in sight; here on these occasions we used to discuss the merits, courage, and exploits of our enemies. I remember on one occasion Captain Ermalaev, of ours, expressed himself nearly as follows to his brother officers:—

"The Englishmen go and return on the sea, but there is no fear that they will reach Sevastopol; they would be afraid to try; let them only try on land, and we would give it them in fine style. The French, we know, can fight, but the English, if they ever do make war, it's only with savages, in a country a long way off—there, I can't think of the name of it—you must all know—it is the place we were to have gone to had we not been ordered here—we were to have advanced by way of the Caucasus. There, I have it at the tip of my tongue! You know, Ivanov! No, I cannot remember the name of the place!"

"I think it was called India," said Stepanov.

"Yes, that's it," caught up Ermalaev. "They are afraid of us! Only let them try, we'll soon send them back again."

A number of men by this time had surrounded the officers, and were standing uncovered in the midday sun. Ermalaev asked them, "Well, my lads, do you think we shall beat the French and English?"

"Yes, sir; if we could only meet them we would soon show them what we are made of."

"That's right, my lads! You see all this business is because these Christians stand up for the dog of a Turk, who impales and boils all our brethren."

"Yes, but how is that, sir, that these people stand up for the Turks and their wickedness?"

"Why, my lads, you see the Turkish Sultan has promised them a piece of Christian land. No, God will defend us in our holy cause. These English don't believe in God! Not long since they attacked a monastery![3] and what do you think was the result? Why, all their shot rebounded, because it was a holy place! But they could not understand that."

The men listened to the words of their captain with great attention; and when he told them that the English had taken the bells from the monastery, they remarked that most probably guns would be made of them to be used in the Crimea or else-

---

3. The monastery of Solovetzki, in the White Sea.

where against the Russians. The worthy captain concluded by saying that "We must all fight for Holy Russia."

To which one and all answered,—"If you don't hang back, we will hold our own." This is a pretty good specimen of the kind of conversation carried on between the men and the officers who have risen from the ranks in the Russian army.

At this time all the Russian papers were full of the sufferings of the Christians in the East. The soldiers even grumbled that they were left in idleness while their comrades were gaining victories [4] on the Danube. I learnt, however, the real state of things in the Principalities from an officer of the 10th division. The troops in the Crimea were dissatisfied too with many things. In the first place, the rations were very indifferent; for Prince Menschikoff, though no doubt a very clever man, was a very unfit commander-in-chief. During five months he never once showed the slightest interest as to the manner in which the men were fed, nor did he ever inspect the cook-houses, which he ought to have done, as what follows will show:—

The commanders of regiments, taking advantage of the indifference of the prince to the comforts of the soldiers (for in the Russian army it is absolutely necessary that they should be looked after), took very little care that their men were well fed, but were at great pains to fill their pockets with gold. Truly provisions at this time were dearer than in ordinary times, still good meat could be bought in the market for five or six *kopecks* [5] per pound, and by taking a large quantify the price would be about one *kopeck* less; at the same time the colonel of our regiment was paying, or rather pretended to be paying, at the rate of seven *kopecks* per pound for a very inferior quality of meat, greatly to his own and the contractor's profit, while the poor soldiers were the sufferers. The man to whom the command of our regiment was entrusted was Major-General Volkhoff; he would never allow the officers in charge of companies to purchase provisions for their men when they could be obtained at a cheaper rate and of

---

4. Such victories!

5. About two and a half *kopecks* make one penny.

a better quality, thereby saving a few *kopecks* out of the provision sum to add to the poor pay of our ill-used, ill-fed men; but even when in want of money the colonels of regiments will even take money from the pay of the soldiers, under the pretence of improving their diet.

The following is a statement of the pay and emoluments of a Russian soldier:—He receives ninety *kopecks* for four months' service (about 3s.), of which, however, he never gets more than sixty *kopecks*, nor even that if his colonel has thought his diet required improvement. The rest of the money goes for various stoppages: there is 1½ *kopecks* for the barber of the company; about three *kopecks* for an image of some saint belonging to the regiment, before which a lamp is supposed to he continually burning; then the men have to find their own caps, and they are charged a percentage for changing the money, which is usually paid in twenty-five or fifty *rouble* notes. Besides this he gets ninety *kopecks* a year to supply himself with the necessary things to clean his arms and accoutrements. A corporal receives one *rouble* fifteen *kopecks* (about 3s. 10d.) every four months, and a sergeant-major three *roubles* (about 10s.), of course subject to the same stoppages as the soldier.

Besides their pay, each soldier receives the leather for two pairs of boots a year, but he must make them himself or pay for the making; a suit of uniform every two years, and a grey great-coat every three years; coarse linen for three shirts every year, and for the lining of their uniform; this linen of the worst possible quality. All the articles of clothing provided by the Government must be worn the full time, and, to enable the men to keep their things in order, a certain sum is allowed every year to the men for repairs; but during the four years I served in the Russian army, I never saw or heard of a soldier receiving this money. What then becomes of it is the natural question. It goes into the colonel's pocket. If a man in charge of a company should ever dare ask about all these things, he will soon find himself struck off the list of captains, and turned adrift.

I cannot help relating here a circumstance that occurred, and which will show the way in which peculation *i.e.* carried on. In the commissariat stores at Sevastopol there was a large quantity of salt beef that, on account of the length of time it had been in salt and the little care that had been used in salting, had become totally unfit for human food. The naval authorities of the town refused to receive it for their men, and in consequence it was thrown upon the hands of the commissariat officers, for in Russia nothing belonging to the Government is supposed to be spoilt. The colonel of our regiment, for his own profit, ordered a board of officers to report that the said salt beef was fit for food; which of course was done, and this beef that had been condemned by the naval authorities was given to our men, When it was cooked not a soldier would even try it, as the smell was overpowering, so that I could not approach the camp-kettle in which it was boiled.

The next day the soldiers were minus their dinner and supper, till at last, conquered by hunger, they ventured to eat it, and we sent per company to the hospital from three to five men daily, who were suffering from diseases caused by the use of unwholesome food. The colonel tried to soak it in water, but it was of no avail; he then tried vinegar, with the like results; till at last he was obliged to order it to be thrown away and to make good the deficiency out of his own pocket; but even then I doubt whether he was a loser by the transaction.

This is the way the poor soldiers are treated, and it is not to be supposed that the case is different under the very nose of the Emperor; though with a good commander the men are better treated. The poor fellows suffer in silence their hard fate, trusting in God, and saying that, if they are called upon to undergo hardships, they still form part of the Army of the Cross, Sometimes, however, when the colonel of a regiment or his officers wear out the patience of those most patient of all creatures their soldiers, they will in times of peace rush from the ranks and tear the epaulettes off their shoulders, or even strike them; of course these men are made examples of, but their tyrant is disgraced. From the same cause the Russian officers fall victims in action, not to the balls of the enemy, but to those of their own men, which will account for the losses of the Russians in officers in all their battles (one regiment at Inkerman lost forty-five officers, having only five left in the whole regiment).

On the 15th of June I saw for the first time a slight engagement at sea, though at a great distance from us. Every day six ships cruised outside the harbour of Sevastopol, and in case of a calm or contrary wind steamers were despatched to tow them into the harbour. No ships ever remained outside the harbour but once, and then a vessel got aground in Sandy Bay, where she lay two days till steamers got her off. On the day in question three screw steamers were seen on the horizon to the eastward, when the following five steamers were ordered to get up steam, *viz. Vladimir, Gromonosetz, Elbrouz, Danube*, and *Khersonese*, and give chase; the steamer *Odessa* was already at sea. The other vessels outside the harbour also bore down upon the three strangers. The whole of our encampment was out upon the hills above the village of Utchkuevka, while the boulevard near the monument of Kosarsky and every other available spot were crowded with spectators; Prince Menschikoff was on the library. Admiral Panfiloff was entrusted with the command of the expedition.

The *Vladimir* outstripped her companions, and consequently was the first to receive the fire of the enemy; the others however coming up, a general cannonade appeared to begin, but the vessels edged away towards the north, and the great distance prevented our seeing anything more of the affair. At last our vessels were seen returning, followed by those of the enemy. I heard that the *Vladimir* lost ten men and received three shots through the sides; of the others I heard nothing, as in Russia it is very difficult to know what is passing around one. I heard, however, from some naval officers, that the admiral lost his self-command, and tried to fire through the *Vladimir*,

The Prince had ordered them to go at full speed on leaving Sevastopol, and that ship being the fastest soon outstripped the others, while the admiral ordered his vessel to slacken speed. They also told me that the firing of the English ships was better than that of the French. On the heights every one began to re-joice, saying that our ships had taken those of the enemy, which they were towing into the harbour; but as they approached we found the reverse to be the true state of the case, as evidently the vessels that left Sevastopol in the morning were flying before the allied squadron.

In the *Invalide* and other papers there were continually arti-cles stating that the Allies were preparing to make a descent in the Crimea for the purpose of destroying Sevastopol, which, it was said, presented too many difficulties to attack it from the sea. In this case I cannot understand why Menschikoff occupied himself so little with fortifications of the south side. The tower on the Malakhoff hill was finished on the 18th of August. It was built of stone, and of two stories; on the upper story were five guns, two twenty-four pounders and three sixteen pound-ers, while on the lower story were only loopholes for musketry. Besides this tower to the south of Oushakoff ravine, an earthen battery of twelve guns had been constructed, as well as another of eight guns behind the sailors' barracks. These works were not connected in any way. The batteries were connected by a dry wall one and a half foot thick and three feet high, without any ditch and with earth thrown up on the outside; the former of these batteries was a stone tower mounting three guns, and the other mounted about fifteen. On the north side had been added a masked battery between Fort Constantine and the tower of Volkhoff. These were the only additions made to the fortifica-tions before the 13th of September, and these were done by the gangs of convicts of the town.

On the 30th of August the 16th division arrived from Odessa with three field batteries of twelve guns each; the strength of this division of sixteen battalions was about 14,000 men and 540 artillerymen. About the same time four regiments of Cossacks arrived, each about 800 men strong.

About the end of August Totleben arrived at Sevastopol for the purpose of defending the town. On his arrival Menschikoff invited him to examine the existing defences and give his opinion on them. Totleben afterwards told the Prince that he would take the town in three hours with two divisions of infantry and field artillery. This answer is said not to have pleased the old diplomatist.

During the five months I had now spent in the Crimea I had only twice seen Prince Menschikoff while under arms, and both these occasions were attended with accidents of a serious nature. On one occasion he inspected our brigade with the 4th and 5th Light Batteries, the 6th battalion of Sappers, and the 12th battery of Horse Artillery. He rode up to us with a frown on his brow, which was not encouraging to the soldier. We marched past in files of companies at a quick march, and then in columns, after which the battery of horse artillery was ordered to advance at a gallop, then halt, and unlimber! But as the ground was on the incline, the horses could not stop the guns; two drivers fell and were crushed under the wheels. There was a large assemblage of spectators on the ground, as so large a body of troops had never before been seen near Sevastopol, and at the sight of the corpses of these two unfortunate men cries of pity were heard from all sides of the crowd, which appeared greatly to affect Menschikoff.

Thus ended our first inspection. Another time we were led by the prince to the mouth of the river Belbek, where he placed us in a position to oppose a descent of the Allies, which proves that the descent was fully expected, and in this place, The horse of one of his *aides-de-camp* stumbled and fell, and as the *aide-de-camp* had a drawn sword in his hand, he fell upon it, and died of the wound in about four hours. These events do not appear very significant compared with those grand events that were to follow; but the Russian soldier is very superstitious, and on seeing these two accidents all exclaimed, "This man will never do to command us, for he has nothing but ill-luck."

It was evident that the soldiers did not like Menschikoff, as was shown after the battle of Alma. He never interfered in anything, but left every arrangement to the men under his command, who were consequently able to fill their pockets with impunity. In the mean time the general of division frequently inspected us, and drilled the men in marching without ever taking the trouble to ascertain whether the men knew how to load or fire their pieces, or anything about skirmishing, which are absolutely necessary for every man to know, in order to be of use in war-time. But the Russian generals, or at least a large portion of them, seem to think that if their men can march well, with their toes pointed and their bodies inflexible, the main object is gained. But it has been of late repeatedly proved by experience that this is not enough.

During the summer we had a gay time of it in the town—balls, theatre, promenades on Sundays and holidays, when the band played on the boulevards, though I must say that the naval officers enjoyed more of these pleasures than we did, as they were better known and more considered than we were as officers of the line.

CHAPTER 2

The Allies Arrive

On the 13th of September there was a rumour among the officers that an enormous fleet of the enemy's vessels had appeared off Cape Lucula, and that on board the ships a large body of troops had been remarked. Many of the younger officers expressed extravagant joy at the idea that God had given our enemies over into our hands; the soldiers were also rejoiced at the news; they were burning with impatience to meet the enemy face to face, as well as for a change in their monotonous lives. Some few of the officers became sick, and required to be sent to the hospital, but the number of these was small. I must say that I looked forward to fleshing my maiden sword with pleasure, and hastened towards the enemy with my comrades, true servants of the Tsar and Russia, though I felt bitterly at the time that in upholding the cause of despotism I was not fighting for my own country, but against it. Many of the officers addressed their men in terms nearly as follows:—

Now, children,[1] the good time has come at last, though we have been obliged to wait some time for it; now we will not disgrace our Russian land; we'll drive back the enemy, and please Batushka [2] the Tsar; then we can return

---

1. The term children is often applied to a body of men from a superior; in the original Russian it is "*rebiata*."
2. "Batushka" means father and is a term of respect aplied to priests &c.

to our homes with the laurels we shall have earned.

For my own part I almost wished that we might be defeated, to see the effect upon these gentlemen, and what they would then say. Truly the moral feeling of the troops was very high at this time; even the sick in the hospitals begged to be allowed to meet the enemy, saying, it was better to die on the field of battle than to rot in bed. There is no doubt that the men had full confidence in their officers, who they expected would set them an example of daring and heroic deeds; but, alas! Their confidence proved to have been misplaced. Those who were quiet in their demeanour, and said little about what they thought of doing in the hour of danger, proved the first on the field of battle; while the boasters were for the most part to be found in the rear.

The 4th battalion of our regiment, with the 3rd battalion of the regiment of Chasseurs of Borodino, advanced at 4 p. m. to the river Katcha to occupy that position, and formed the advanced guard of the army. The following troops were brought across the harbour from the south side of Sevastopol:—1st brigade of the 14th division with its artillery, and four reserve battalions of the 13th division. The next morning at 10 o'clock our regiment was drawn up before the camp in readiness to march on the Alma, which was the position chosen by Prince Menschikoff to defeat the forces of the enemy and drive him into the sea. It was generally reported that in any case the enemy would not be allowed to approach the town, and that the first battle was to be given at the Alma, the second on the Katcha, and, if necessary, the third and most desperate on the Belbek; these three positions were said to have been chosen by Prince Menschikoff himself.

Before we moved off the ground, Ensign P——, a countryman and fellow patriot, asked me what I thought of matters. I said, I thought the Allies knew all that was going on in our camp, and what our actual strength was; but I remarked that I had little confidence in our leaders, as they were too fond of boasting, especially when under the influence of the bottle; that our duty nevertheless called upon us to aid them. At 11 a.m. we moved, and by the time we reached the Katcha a great many men had fallen out from fatigue, not that the distance was great, but that the men were unaccustomed to march. We, however, marched cheerfully along; the band played occasionally, but more frequently the singers and dancers [3] performed before the battalion.

We reached the Katcha at 5 p.m., where we bivouacked for the night. It was not very comfortable, as it rained all night, and we were unprovided with tents or any other field equipage. Everybody had said that it was useless to overburden ourselves, as we should beat the enemy out of the Crimea and return in a day or two.

On the morning of the 15th, about five o'clock, we moved from the Katcha, and halted on the heights about two miles before reaching the Alma. This morning's march was not quite so cheerful as that of the day before, as the rain had not improved the state of the road, and, to add to our discomfort, we met large trains of wagons containing stores, spare ammunition, sick men belonging to the 16th division, encamped on the Alma, which was ordered to retire to the Katcha. This meeting rather damped our spirits and shook our confidence.

On reaching our position on the heights one of the most beautiful sights it was ever my lot to behold lay before us. The whole of the allied fleet was lying off the salt lakes to the south of Eupatoria, and at night their forest of masts was illuminated with various-coloured lanterns. Both men and officers were lost in amazement at the sight of such a large number of ships together, especially as many of them had hardly ever seen the sea before. The soldiers said, "Behold, the infidel has built another holy Moscow on the waves," comparing the masts of the ships to the church-spires of that city. The officers began to speculate that such a fleet must have brought at least eighty thousand men, and were not quite so sure of victory as they were two days before.

But as it was necessary to keep up the spirits of the men, some

---

3. There is a buffoon, who is one of the soldiers generally attached to each company. —H. D. S.

of the officers, pointing to the stately fleet, said, "Well, children, there are plenty of ships, but only let the troops land, and then we shall see; if they do outnumber us—Russians never stop to count, but cut down all before them! Besides, a great number of the ships we see contain provisions and stores."

"Yes, sir, but still he must be pretty strong!"

"Never fear, my lads! We are fighting for a just cause, and God will help us."

I must say that the troops were all impatience to engage the enemy.

On this day was performed a daring action at Sevastopol. The greater part of the allied fleet was covering the landing of the troops; two vessels were left to watch the mouth of the harbour, while a few others were cruising off the coast. Early in the morning, Captain Popoff, having previously obtained permission from Admiral Korniloff, got up steam on board his ship, the *Taman*, and during a dense fog effected his escape through the cruisers, and after doing considerable damage to the transports of the Allies, got safe and sound into Nicolaieff, carrying with him, it is reported, a Turkish transport. What induces me to believe this story is, that when we left Sevastopol I saw the *Taman* in the harbour, and when I returned on the 21st to the north side she was gone; and upon inquiry some naval men related the above.

In the evening the general of our division, Lieutenant-General Kiriakoff, came up to us; our colonel asked him what was going on yonder, pointing to the allied fleets. The general said that about 8000 men had been disembarked, and that he had asked permission of the prince to drive them into the sea with his brigade, He spoke loud that the men might hear him, and they said among themselves, "What a fine fellow is our general of division!"—but, alas! When proved he was found wanting. About the village of Bourliouk there were a great many vineyards and orchards with the fruit just ripe, to which the soldiers helped themselves very liberally, for in Russia grapes are unheard-of luxuries among the lower orders.

On the 16th we still occupied the same position. In the evening an artilleryman of our brigade, 5th light field battery, brought a report to General Kiriakoff that in the village of Ul-ukul there was a party of the enemy's marauders, whom he had seen himself while on a foraging party. Kiriakoff ordered our colonel to furnish a party consisting of one subdivision and twenty-four riflemen. All the officers of the regiment crowded round the general and colonel to learn the particulars from the artilleryman, who was relating the strength and position of the enemy. When the adjutant of the regiment announced to the colonel that the men were ready, he turned to us and asked who would volunteer for the service. I answered to the call, and Lieutenant K—— was ordered to join the party, as he belonged to the rifles of the battalion.

The orders we received were to take as many prisoners as possible. The village was about eight versts from the position we occupied, and close to the shore. I started with my command about a quarter past six, with the artilleryman for a guide, who was on horseback. The village in question had been deserted by its inhabitants. I advanced cheerfully towards my object, and considered myself very fortunate in having the command of this small expedition, as success would place me high in the opinion of my commanding officers.

Notwithstanding the distance, which was not small, we rapidly approached the village, where we remarked lights in several of the huts; these, our guide assured us, were the lights of the marauders, as there were no inhabitants in the village, and these lights could proceed from no one but the enemy. My heart beat high at this moment, and I considered the victory already mine. We reached the first village. There were three of the same name- upper, middle, and lower. Nothing disturbed the stillness of the night but the dreadful howling of the dogs that had remained about their old haunts, deserted by their Tatar masters.

The night was so dark that a man could not be distinguished at the distance of three paces. We advanced to within two musket-shots of the lights, when I stopped and threw out skirmishers. We then began to move on with all possible caution, so that the enemy might not remark our approach, as I wished to fulfil my orders and take them all alive. We moved on for another thousand yards, when I resolved to call a council of war as to the best mode of proceeding. Lieutenant K—— was of opinion that it would be better to open fire upon two sides of the village, while the cadet E——, who was promoted to the rank of officer for the battle of Inkerman, advised to open fire upon the village, and then charge into it, I overruled these opinions in consequence of the orders I had received to make prisoners and not kill the men.

To carry out this, I advised that one of us, with a few men, should advance to reconnoitre and ascertain whether or not this was really a party of the enemy. Should it prove to be, he was to retire and give information to the rest of our party, that we might concert measures. If the reconnoitring party were discovered, a shot fired was to be a signal for the rest to advance and begin a hand-to-hand combat. This appeared to me the best way to perform my duty. I then proposed to the officers with me that one should undertake this duty. As nobody seemed willing, I resolved, after some little consideration, to go myself. I gave the command to Lieutenant K—— in case I should not return, with orders to advance at the first shot fired.

Our hesitation at this time is not at all extraordinary, considering that not one of us had ever seen a shot fired in earnest, and now we were rushing on an unknown and unseen danger, feeling that if we were overpowered we had no one near to support us. I picked out two men that I considered the most to be depended upon. We began to descend the slope towards the village, crawling on our bellies, and I must confess that I felt a strange sensation of cold; my heart beat faster at the thought that in a few minutes we should be engaged in a mortal struggle. I tried, however, to hide this feeling, of which I was ashamed, from my men. After all, I don't think it was cowardice—it might have been the effect of the cold night-dew through which we were crawling.

We approached nearer and nearer, till at last I observed the shine of a bayonet through the darkness that appeared to belong to a sentry evidently posted near a house, from the windows of which we could see lights. What could this mean? Had the enemy occupied the village in force? This I thought was not possible, as our general ought to have known it, and sent a stronger party. Again, it could not be a single company that thus ran the risk of being cut off; yet I could not imagine that if they were simply marauders they would have posted a sentry at the entrance of the village. I did not know what to do. I could not return, for in that case I should be obliged to confess that I ran away from one man, for I could see no more through the darkness, and whether he was an Englishman, a Frenchman, or a Turk, I could not tell.

To return would stamp me for a coward, and I would never give a Russian an opportunity to call a Pole a coward. While I was thus reasoning with myself, one of the men with me, as we were lying on the ground, said, "If you'll allow me, sir, I'll go and see who they are in the village."

I told him that if he would remain quietly in his place I would go myself, for, as an officer, I thought it my duty to go first; but when I had crawled a short distance I trembled from head to foot, as I heard footsteps approaching, and tried to conceal myself behind a bush. As the man approached I saw a sentry—of what nation think ye ?—Russian! I could hardly believe my eyes. Was it possible that a Russian picket could be here unknown to General Kiriakoff?

Jumping up from my hiding-place, I greatly disturbed the nerves of the sentry, and asked him what regiment he belonged to; "The infantry regiment of Minsk, sir," said he."

"How many of you are there in the village?"

"The 2nd battalion and four guns, sir."

I thought our general of division must have been beside himself to send me on such a fool's errand, and, had it not been for the caution used in approaching the village, few of us would have returned to tell the tale, for the night was so dark that at a short distance it would be impossible to know friend from foe. I asked where the commander of the battalion lived, and was shown the house where the lights were visible, which would have been our target had we commenced firing. I then called my two men, and the patrol conducted us to the house of the commander. I told how I came there, and that not very far off was a party of my men awaiting my signal to rush upon the village. He was kind enough to send and invite Lieutenant K—— into his house, while we ordered our men to pile their arms and rest a little.

Upon inquiry I found the regiment of Minsk occupied the village in alternate battalions with four guns, by order of General Kiriakoff of our division. This will give a good idea of the generals we had in the Crimea at the battle of the Alma. The order to occupy this village was entirely forgotten when we were sent with a handful of men to attack it. On the way back I made the artilleryman give up his horse to me, forcing him to walk, as a punishment for leading us on such a wild-goose chase, and we all began to feel tired, for we had done five and a half miles in one and a quarter hours. We got back to our bivouac at 11 p.m. I went to report our adventures to the colonel, who sent me to General Kiriakoff, whom I could not see, as he was with Prince Menschikoff. Turning towards the sea, I had the splendid spectacle of the allied fleet, with its various coloured lights.

On the morning of the 17th I went to the general to make my report of my last night's adventure. He answered—"Ah! Yes, I had forgotten; that'll do." It appears to me extraordinary how a man in such circumstances could be so negligent; besides, this was the only village on the coast between the Alma and the Katcha, so that one would suppose it impossible to forget that it was occupied by a part of our army, situated as it was in our rear. Luckily for me I used precaution, for, had I opened fire and escaped with my life, I should have been reduced to the ranks, or perhaps sent to Siberia. In the Russian service it is impossible for a general to be in fault when only a captain of a company is in question. Russia is not the free country that England is, where a free press exists, and where every man can appeal for justice to public opinion, no matter who may be his oppressors. God only knows the amount of injustice that is suffered in this way.

On this day the Sub-Lieutenant Kar—— arrived to join his regiment. He had been acting as *aide-de-camp* to Major B——, also of our regiment, who was commandant at Eupatoria, where there were about 200 invalids from different regiments in the Crimea, who were sent thither for the benefit of sea-bathing.

Lieutenant Kar—— related that he had seen the enemy's flag of truce, and what occurred at Eupatoria during the night; as near as I can remember, his account was as follows:—

In the afternoon boats came in with flags of truce from the English and French. All the officers of the Allies were in full uniform, and asked for the Commandant, who presented himself in his grey soldier's coat. Twenty-four hours were given to clear out the place. What happened on that momentous night is beyond description. All the inhabitants crowded the streets and wharfs, and nobody could be persuaded to execute the orders of the commandant, who directed that all the stores should be destroyed, and that the flour in the magazines should be mixed with lime, of which there was a large quantity in the place. He required also transport, to carry away his sick and baggage, and he could get no one to attend to his requisitions.

Many of the inhabitants were desirous of leaving the place, but, not having the means, applied to the commandant for assistance; while he could not find the necessary conveyance for his own men and their baggage. Everything was disorder; shouts and cries resounded on all sides, while everybody seemed inclined to do nothing; in fact, a perfect chaos reigned in the place throughout the night. At length Major B——, with the troops under his command, and the inhabitants with such effects as they could save, moved in a confused mass towards Simpheropol. It was extraordinary that the town was not fired; but it is probable that the commandant thought it useless, as the Tatar

37

inhabitants, who remained, would have soon extinguished the fire.

On the morning of the 18th General Kiriakoff ordered out the men who did the duty of skirmishers, and instructed them in the art of capturing guns from the enemy, which appeared easy enough when the gun was placed in the open field without any one near, but I rather doubt its efficacy during an action; at least I have never heard of its succeeding in the Crimea. I remarked to one of my comrades, an old schoolfellow, at the time, that it would be well to ascertain whether there could be any possibility of the enemy capturing our own guns. The instruction was as follows:—

Two sections of skirmishers, forty-eight men, were to rush upon four guns. The first section was to make for the horses, and bayonet the men, while the second section was to bayonet the men at the guns, seize them, turn their muzzles towards the enemy, and try to drag them off, while in that case others were to come to their assistance. This was a very pretty manoeuvre when the guns were standing quietly, but during an action it would not be quite so easy.

"In this way I captured four guns during the campaign in Poland," said General Kiriakoff. The soldiers expected, to use a Russian idiom, to see him snatch stars from heaven on the day of battle!

At 11 a.m. we took up a position on the river Alma pointed out by Captain Joloboff of the general staff. Our regiment was on the left flank of the position, in the second line; before us were the reserves of the 13th division— General Oslonovich; in short, the army was in the second fighting order, in the form of a chessboard, according to the Russian tactics, in two lines with reserves in the third. While here I walked over the ground, and carefully examined the position occupied by our army. The village of Bourliouk was sacked, and our men used to go there and bring away pillows, feather-beds, household utensils of various kinds, boards, doors, &c. It was grievous to look at this village, as it had been deserted by its inhabitant, who left everything in their houses. At this time I had seen little of war. We constructed for ourselves huts of the branches of trees, and luxuriated in fruit, of which we found great quantities in the gardens, especially grapes.

On the morning of the 19th we were ordered to move across the river in half strength, *i.e.* all the odd men in the battalion as they stood in the ranks were to go, while even numbers were to remain and form another battalion; thus we had two battalions instead of one, or a brigade that looked like a division. This was a plan of General Kiriakoff for the purpose of increasing his strength, approved of by Prince Menschikoff, who remarked that if the men stood in the ranks at double the ordinary distance from each other they would appear still more numerous! We now learnt that our general had offered to make a reconnaissance on the enemy with his brigade (the 2nd brigade of the 17th division), with No. 4 light field battery, the 2nd brigade (Hussars) of the 6th division of cavalry, nine *sotnias* of Don Cossacks, and one Cossack battery. We advanced about two versts, when we formed into fighting order, the regiment of Borodino on the right in columns of battalions in two lines, the regiment Taroutine on the left in the same order as that of Borodino, with the battery No. 4 in the centre, while the Hussars covered the right flank, and the Cossacks our left flank. In this order we moved slowly towards the heights above the river Boulganak, below which we halted in a position entirely hidden from the enemy; so much so that we could not see the skirmish between the cavalry of the two armies that took place on the other side of the hills.

As our cavalry was returning, General Kiriakoff ordered the battery to open fire as soon as the enemy's cavalry showed itself above the hills. During the preceding night General Chaletzky had gone out on a reconnoitring expedition with two squadrons of hussars in white jackets, of which the commander of the battery knew nothing, as all our cavalry wore the grey great-coat.

By some accident these two white-jacketed squadrons showed themselves last over the hill at same distance from the others. Lieutenant-Colonel Kondratieff, taking them for the enemy, opened fire on them, and sent them one round shot from each of his eight guns. Lieutenant-Colonel Kondratieff cannot be blamed for this, as he only obeyed the orders of his general, who probably had forgotten all about the reconnaissance of General Chaletzky, or he ought to have warned the commander of the battery not to fire into his own men.

General Chaletzky, a Polish Tatar by birth, galloped round the regiment of Borodino with his sword drawn, and at full speed made towards Lieutenant-Colonel Kondratieff. We fully expected to see a tragic end to this affair, when General Kiriakoff galloped up from the other side, and arrived just in time to prevent mischief; he endeavoured to pacify the hussar, at least he saved the life of the commander of the battery, This was another of the freaks of the commander of our division, from which there were seven men killed and wounded. With the Hussars there was a French colonel, a prisoner, who had mistaken them for the cavalry of the allied army, and only discovered his mistake when too late. I think I saw him driven off the field in a carriage after the battle of Alma.

Unfortunately for Russia there are too many men elevated to posts of power and influence that are utterly incapable of governing the machines entrusted to them; for a Russian soldier forms part of a machine, which is composed of enormous masses of men that never have thought and never will think, They are oppressed with blows and ill-treatment; their understanding is kept down by their servitude and the severe laws to which they are subjected. Sometimes a man more sprightly than his comrades will try to solve some knotty point, but he soon loses himself in the mystery, and only escapes by concluding that, as he knows nothing about it, it is the business of God and the Emperor, but none of his! All wonderful human inventions he sets down to the power of enchantment, without trying to find out their causes. It is an axiom in the Russian army "that the powers of reasoning are not expected in the ranks;" and when this rule is broken through by an aspiring wight he is frequently rewarded for it by a severe corporal punishment.

In consequence of this a Russian soldier is generally dirty in his habits. Frequently you see him bent like an old man, with his head down. He feels his position, but he has not the moral energy to attempt an escape from his tyrants. A leader could easily be found, but they would be afraid to follow, and the leader would be consigned to Siberia. A Russian soldier is perhaps the most unhappy being in the world. When the Emperor inspected our regiment at St. Petersburg in 1853, he remarked that the men kept their eyes fixed on the ground, and did not appear in good spirits. The captains of companies were blamed for this, though I was burning to explain to the colonel why the men looked dejected. However I remembered Siberia, and held my peace. Captain Gorieff flogged one of his men to make him laugh! He happened to be a man who seldom or never laughed—one of those morose-looking fellows that one meets sometimes. It is hardly to be credited, but after receiving one hundred lashes the man managed to get up a laugh, though I must say it bore a great affinity to the sobs that followed this effort.

This is Russian justice! The outward appearance is all that is necessary for the chiefs. If a man has eaten nothing for two days he is still expected to laugh! Frequently the pork used for the preparation of the evening meal of *casha* is in a state wholly unfit for human food; even dogs will not touch it sometimes; but the soldier must eat that or none—if any wight should dare to complain, he is flogged. He, the soldier, frequently has not another shirt besides the one on his back, which he cannot change for purposes of cleanliness.[4] Besides these evils, every man, from a corporal to a general of division, knocks him about *à volonté,* so that sometimes he loses several teeth at a blow. He also suffers severe punishment if he is seen with his clothes torn or untidy; and yet his miserable pay will not allow him to provide himself with

---

4. It was remarked nevertheless of the Russian troops killed at the Alma, how clean their linen was always found.—Ed.

needles and thread for the purpose of repairing his things. After all this he is told to laugh, and, if he does not obey, is punished! I wonder who could laugh under these circumstances! Doubtless the Emperor knows nothing of all this, as it is kept studiously from him. Everyone is well aware that to show brutality to a soldier before him would be certain ruin. The guards, artillery, sappers, and rifles, being all picked men, are better treated than the men of the line.

I quitted the corps of cadets, where I was educated, in the year 1851, and at once joined my regiment. To my misfortune I found the captain, and all the other officers of the company to which I belonged, *bombons, i.e.* men from the ranks, and their treatment of the men disgusted me from the beginning, while they assured me that I should never be able to do anything with the soldiers unless I swore at them in the most filthy manner, and used my fists as they did. Because I would not and could not agree with them, saying that a Russian soldier was a man and ought to be treated as such, I was honoured with the title of the young lady with white hands. I was, however, determined to prove that my theory was as good, if not better, than theirs, and soon brought my men to an excellent state of discipline by words alone, and. by rewarding those who conducted themselves well, which encouraged them to do still better, and the others to emulate them; rarely indeed was I driven to the extreme measure of punishing a man, which I always did before his comrades; in this extremity the men themselves generally agreed that I was right.

The result of my system was that I was generally cheerfully obeyed. When my comrades discovered that I could do my duty with kindness, they began to say that I was by far too familiar with the men and that they would lose all respect for me; whereas the men of the other companies soon began to envy those who were under my orders. As a proof of the efficacy of my system, I can only state that I was always defended by my men in any danger, while the severe officers were the first to fall from the balls of their own soldiers in the heat of an action.

I cannot help here relating an anecdote that occurred in our regiment: Captain Poklonsky had a soldier in his company of the name of Choulkoff, who was continually being punished on drill, almost every day. From having once got into that habit, the poor fellow was so timid and nervous that he always expected, and was seldom disappointed, of his fifty strokes across the back with a drum or other stick.

One day Captain Poklonsky ordered this miserable wretch his portion, when, to the surprise of all, he said he had a request to make to the captain. On inquiry, he said that he wanted permission to take off his clothes before he was beaten, as it had happened so frequently to him that they were beginning to give way under it; the humane captain ordered an addition to the former number of blows to be given to the man with his clothes on, for daring to presume to ask such a favour.

To return to the subject. As the enemy remained on the river Boulganak, we retired to our position on the Alma about 6 p.m. On our left flank they were building a kind of telegraph or lookout, at which several shots were fired by the fleets evidently for the purpose of getting the range; many of our officers laughed at this as the shots fell short, and none louder than Captain Volkhoff, to whom I remarked that this was a bad sign, and that I should not be at all surprised if on the morrow we were roughly handled from the sea. He remarked that all the shots fell short; but my predictions were too true.

During our reconnaissance it would have been easy for the Allies to have done us a great deal of harm, and even to have made the greater part of our column prisoners, or at least to have rushed pell-mell with us up to the position occupied by the army, where the artillery could not fire without killing their own people, Of course I know nothing of the reasons that prevented the allied commanders from attempting that coup; they thought probably there was an ambush in the village of Bourliouk, but our generals would not think of such a thing.

As it became dark we could see plainly enough the enemy's fires on the river Boulganak. I lay down in my hut of branches, and tried to sleep, but in vain, notwithstanding the fatigues of the preceding day. I rose about 3 o'clock; it was still dark; the soldiers were collected around the huge fires they had kindled with the plunder of the village of Bourliouk, and orders had been given to burn all the huts of branches, which added to the number of fires. After a short time I went up the hill (for our battalion was stationed in a ravine), to take a peep at the bivouac of the allied armies. Little, however, was to be seen but the fires, and now and then a dark shadow as someone moved past them. All was still and had little appearance of the coming strife.

There were both armies lying, as it were, peacefully, side by side. How many, or who, would be sent to their last account, it would be impossible to say. The question involuntarily thrust itself upon me, should I be one of that number? While thus buried in reflection on the uncertainty of human life, my comrade Römer approached me. Römer was a good fellow, but had fallen into misfortune for having too freely spoken the truth in 1849; after passing a year and a half in prison he had served as a private soldier four years. He related to me anecdotes of the war in the Caucasus, where he had served five years, before he got into trouble, as a cadet. We exchanged addresses, so that, in case either of us was killed, the other was to write to inform his family of the event.

In the Russian army there are no nominal returns of the killed and wounded, so that, unless one happens to be a general or a colonel at least, it is very difficult to ascertain the fate of an officer who has ceased writing to his friends; the fate of a soldier it is next to impossible to learn. Our precautions were however useless, for a better fate has been reserved for us both. We then drew near a circle of soldiers, when a veteran remarked that no good would come to them today.

"Why?"

"As if you don't know as well as I do! we are to have no vodka, and how can we fight without it?"

The others all agreed with him. Truly, in our regiment, the men had no vodka, for our worthy colonel thought it advisable to put the money into his own pocket, remarking that half these fellows will be killed, so it will be only a waste to give them vodka. The canteen-man of our battalion remained on the ground till the action began, when he decamped, leaving a barrel of vodka behind him, as he had no horses for the transport of his goods. Our men, however, soon finished the vodka, and were consequently in high spirits. I can answer for it that none of the other battalions had any spirits. As for the other regiments, I know nothing, nor can I venture an opinion, as I have heard so many conflicting statements on the subject.

CHAPTER 3

The Alma

The position chosen by Prince Menschikoff on the Alma, for the purpose of meeting, and, as he fondly hoped, of defeating the invaders of the Crimea, was a position of great strength: his army was disposed on the heights above the river, the banks of which are very steep and planted with trees on either side, which rendered the passage very difficult. On the right bank of the river there was the village of Bourliouk, with its gardens, stacks of corn, &c. A Tatar village is about one of the worst obstacles that can present itself to the manoeuvring of troops, because the streets are very narrow and crooked, but chiefly because the Tatars and Nogais are in the habit of digging large funnel-shaped holes before their houses, where they store their grain. These holes are generally covered over with planks and a thin layer of earth, so that cavalry or artillery would he thrown into utter confusion if they were to attempt to advance through a village with obstacles like these.

Prince Menschikoff had the following troops under his orders:—

Infantry,

	Battalions.	Guns.
First brigade of the 14th division, with. No. 3 battery of position, and No. 3 light battery.	8	16

The 16th division, with 16th brigade of Artillery No. 1 and 2 light batteries, and No. 2 battery of position.	16	36
Second brigade of 17th division, with the regiment of Moscow (that arrived from Kertch at 8 a.m.), with the 17th brigade of Artillery No. 4 and 5 light batteries, and No. 3 battery of position.	12	24
Reserve battalions of the 13th division.	4	—
The Rifle and Sapper battalions of the 6th corps.	2	—
2 battalions of sailors from Sevastopol with 4 field-pieces	2	4
All together	44	80

It was very amusing to see the advance of the sailors: their four guns were taken out of the condemned ordnance stores at Sevastopol, with carriages tied together in many places with ropes. These guns were each drawn by two miserable horses assisted by eight men, and frequently, where the road was heavy or uphill, the whole battalion had to assist in hauling their guns. This was no doubt an idea of the prince, for, being a naval man, he always showed a greater partiality for sailors than for the regular army; and I have no doubt, had we been successful, these amphibious warriors would have gained all the credit and reaped all the reward.

The cavalry consisted of the 2nd brigade, (Hussars) of the 6th Cavalry division, with the light battery of horse-artillery No. 12, the Don Cossack battery No. 4; all together 16 squadrons and 16 guns; and two regiments, or 16 *sotnias*, of Don Cossacks.

Thus the whole Russian force at the Alma was 44 battalions of infantry, 16 squadrons of cavalry, 16 *sotnias* of Cossacks,[1] and 96 guns, which were disposed as follows:—On the extreme right, in the valley, was stationed the cavalry, with the horse-ar-

1. Taking the battalions at 750 men each, this would give 33,000 infantry and 3400 cavalry, including Cossacks.

tillery; next to them were the battalions of sailors with their four wretched guns. On the right flank there was erected a redoubt, in which was placed the No. 2 battery of position of the 16th artillery brigade; to the right of this redoubt was the regiment of Ouglitz in columns of battalions in two lines, while to the left was the regiment of Kazan in the same order.

These two regiments form the 2nd brigade of the 16th division. Behind them, on the hill, was stationed the 1st brigade of the 16th division as a reserve. To the left of the regiment of Kazan was the regiment of Chasseurs of Borodino (2nd brigade, 17th division), also in columns of battalions and in two lines, while between the regiments of Kazan and Borodino were stationed No. 1 and 2 light batteries of the 16th artillery brigade, which played chiefly on the river and on the village of Bourliouk. To the left of the regiment of Borodino were the four reserve battalions of the 13th division in the front line, and in rear of them our regiment (the regiment of Taroutine, 2nd brigade, 17th division), also in columns. In the rear of our regiment was the regiment of Moscow (1st brigade, 17th division) in reserve.

The chief reserve consisted of the 1st brigade of the 14th division with five batteries of artillery, with the exception however of one battalion of the regiment of Minsk, and four guns that I stumbled so unexpectedly upon in the last chapter. These were still stationed at the village of Ulukul Akles, as it was said, for the purpose of catching marauders, or to prevent a descent in the rear of our army. Our left flank extended to the heights that overlooked the ravine leading up from the river, at about two *versts* from the sea.

The right was under the orders of the commander of the 16th division, Lieutenant-General Kvetzintzky, the centre under Prince Gortchakoff I, and the left under the commander of the 17th division, Lieutenant-General Kiriakoff. The whole army was commanded by Prince Menschikoff.

In conversation with my brother officers I found that it was the general opinion that we should be able to hold this position for at least a week, and the only danger that threatened us was, that the enemy might outflank us on the right of our position.

If I might venture an opinion which I conceived at that time, but dared not express, I should think that our left flank ought not to have been left entirely without artillery, while the ravine that led up to it was quite undefended, and the stone bridge across the river remained undestroyed. If, as was expected, our right flank had been turned, we could easily have changed our front and so held our own. At least it appears to me even now, that with good generalship we might have held the position till night, and then retreated without disgrace.

As we had seen the fires of the allied armies, so we were ready to meet the enemy at daylight.

At half-past 6 a.m. orders were given to send all the wagons to the rear. At 7 the whole regiment was assembled around the tent of the colonel, Major-General Volkhoff, when, in the presence of General Kiriakoff, a holy mass was said to the Virgin Mary for her aid to defeat our enemies. At 9 a. m. the French brought what appeared to us from the hill a large white box, drawn by six horses, which box was placed in front of the village of Al Malamak. The rumour ran through our regiment, and the four battalions of reserve in front of us, that the enemy had brought up a box which was supposed to be filled with gas, "*pour nous asphyxier.*"

"What a barbarous idea!" exclaimed some of the officers. This rumour soon reached the colonel, and, at last, the general commanding the division; when Lieutenant Katansky, who commanded the riflemen of our regiment, proposed to set fire to this mysterious box by means of rockets fired from rifles. There was a great deal of talk, but no one took any measures to ascertain what it was. At last, from simple curiosity, I asked leave of the commander of our battalion, Major Iliashevitch, to go and ascertain what it could mean. Every one of the officers tried to dissuade me, saying that I should be shot from the steamers, or that the box might be connected by galvanic wires. Still, every one of them was burning with impatience to know what it could be.

Without listening to their objections I started to examine this supposed new engine in warfare, and I found it to be a large cubical stone! During this walk I remarked how extremely exposed our left flank was to an attack, and on my return informed General Kiriakoff of my observation, when he sent the 2nd battalion of the regiment of Moscow into the ravine, with orders to hold the bridge and to detach sharpshooters into the gardens on the right bank of the river.

The commander of the left flank had occupied this ground during four days, but had never once taken the trouble to examine the position, to enable him to dispose of the force under his orders to the best advantage.

I expressed my opinion to the major that I thought the stone I had seen was a forerunner of an attack upon our left, where it would be easier to succeed than on the right or centre. Nobody, however, would believe my reasoning, opposing the steepness of the heights on that side, but forgetting the undefended ravine and the absence of artillery. The transporting of this stone I can only account for by supposing that the French, wishing to ascertain whether there were any troops in the village of Al Malamak and to reconnoitre the banks of the river, adopted this ruse as being less likely to expose them than a reconnaissance.

About 11 a. m we could see the columns of the allied army advancing in the most splendid order, with colours flying, drums beating, and bands playing, as if to a review. Soon afterwards an *aide-de-camp* of the prince galloped past our battalion to the general with the information that the enemy was advancing towards the left flank.[2] The general immediately told his *aide-de-camp* to order his horse and six bottles of champagne. At this time the rifle battalion crossed to the right bank of the river, and occupied the village of Bourliouk, the gardens and vineyards around it, with a thick line of sharpshooters; while the battalions in the front threw out skirmishers to occupy the left bank of the river.

---

2. This of course we were able to see, but doubtless Menschikoff gave this hint to General Kiriakoff that he might make some arrangements for meeting the expected attack.

The prince rode up to our battalion, when the general met him, and remarked that it would be as well to have a battery of artillery on the left flank, between the 1st and 2nd battalions of our regiment, "Oh! no, your Excellency, we can stop them with our bayonet." The prince then passed on to the extreme left.

The great fault of Prince Menschikoff was the blind confidence he placed in his generals, from hearing them boast of their past and future exploits. I have heard General Kiriakoff assure him that with his brigade alone he would be more than a match for any two English divisions. "Was not I in the campaign of Poland?" he would add by way of proof.

At 12 a.m. the whole of the allied armies were in full view, and a more magnificent sight man never saw than when, at the distance of about two cannon-shots from us, they began to deploy from marching columns. To the right, as we stood, went the red jackets, and I asked our colonel who they were, and he informed me that they were the English, Upon hearing this many of the officers and most of the men expressed their regret that the English army was going to attack the right and centre. "It would be good fun to fight with them, as, though they may be good sailors, they must be bad soldiers; why, they would have no chance with us on dry land!"

This was an opinion expressed by many on the morning of that day, but I had received my education at the corps of cadets, and knew something of the military tactics and history of the English, and on being asked my opinion I said "that we should see how they fought!" I was obliged to give an evasive answer, for, had I expressed an opinion contrary to theirs, I should have immediately fallen into disgrace, and perhaps been arrested.

The Allies, having formed into order of battle, and thrown out skirmishers, advanced slowly but firmly towards the river. At a distance of about 2000 yards our riflemen opened fire upon the troops advancing towards the village; but the English and French boldly kept the even tenor of their way till the main body was within 1500 yards, and then the skirmishers opened fire. About ten minutes before this a heavy cannonade was opened from the sea, which told very heavily upon the regiments of Minsk and Moscow, and No. 4 Light Battery of our (17th) Artillery brigade. As the enemy's skirmishers approached, our riflemen retired across the river, and, at the same time, the Cossacks set fire to the corn-stacks on the left of the village, from which the flames soon spread to the village itself.

The view of the advancing columns of the enemy, as they approached the burning village, was at this time the most beautiful, as compared to any other time of the day. Now we began to see the danger that threatened our battalion, for four field-guns were brought up to the left-hand side, looking from our position, of the remains of the haystacks, which were still burning. The round-shot began to fly about our heads. At this time the quartermaster-general of the division rode past us, when we all cried out to him that a battery was required here. He replied that he had ordered one to come up from the reserve, but was told that without the orders of Prince Menschikoff they would not move. Here our brave fellows, who were going to perform such wonders, cried out that we must all perish without artillery.

In about twenty minutes a battery came up that engaged the guns of the enemy and took their fire off us, though they still told heavily upon the reserve battalions in front of us, and threw them into such disorder that they began, without any orders, to retire according to the discretion of their general, Oslonovich, for whom there could be no excuse, though for the men there was, as they were all young soldiers. He twice rode up to our general, Kiriakoff, to ask for assistance. The commander of our battalion, Major Iliashevitch, fearing to be picked off by the sharpshooters, would not mount his horse, but stood with his charger between him and the enemy; the colonel of the regiment did the same, but this was more excusable, as he was very aged and infirm, having gained his rank of major-general by length of service.

The commander of the division was also dismounted, having previously sent away all his *aides-de-camp*, so that he might not be. remarked. In fact, he appeared to me to be entirely lost, and not to know where he was or what to do, while shot, shell, and rifle-balls were whistling around him: at least he quite forgot his duty as general of division.[3] At last one of the *aides-de-camp* of General Kiriakoff galloped up and told him that our left flank was turned. Without a word he mounted and rode to the rear.

This was one of the generals to whom was entrusted the marshalling of one of the flanks of the Russian army at the Alma! As the Minié balls began to reach our battalion, the major decided that it was time to retreat. We accordingly left the ravine in which we were stationed and ascended the hill. Here another part of the battle was opened to us. On the right flank the English were pressing on, [4] though not a few of them were left in the river and on its banks. We were all astonished at the extraordinary firmness with which the red jackets, having crossed the river, opened a heavy fire in line upon the redoubt. [5] The regiments of Kazan and Ouglitz were the first Russian troops who felt the sharpness of English bayonets, but the brave islanders, with their thin line, were unshaken in this trial, notwithstanding the masses opposed to them.

The 1st and 2nd battalions of the regiment of Borodino advanced towards the river in skirmishing order towards the left-hand side of the burning village, but they were cut down like corn by the rifle-balls of the advancing English, who crossed the river at this point. The battalions of reserve had long ceased to exist in the *mêlée*. Three battalions of the regiment of Moscow

---

3. While these events were passing, the French had gained the heights, cutting to pieces the 2nd battalion of the regiment of Moscow that alone opposed them; here they were met by the regiment of Minsk and the other three battalions of the regiment of Moscow, with a battery of artillery. But they came too late, as the French were already on the heights and could not be driven back. The French had every advantage in crossing the river, as the trees afforded good shelter, and they had at their service a good stone bridge with little or no opposition.

4. They had crossed the river under a murderous fire of round shot, grape, and musketry; twice they seemed to us to waver at the bridge, but at the third attempt dashed over the bridge and through the river in a body.

5. This was the most extraordinary thing to us, as we had never before seen troops fight in lines of two deep, nor did we think it possible for men to be found with sufficient firmness of morale to be able to attack in this apparently weak formation our massive columns.

were sent to the left flank to oppose the French already on the hill, but notwithstanding the coolness displayed by the colonel of this regiment, Major-General Kourtianoff, he could effect nothing of any importance, as he was sent too late into action. About this time there arrived three battalions of the regiment of Minsk, with a battery of artillery; but all this was too late, as the enemy was allowed to gain the heights almost without opposition, and then they tried to drive him back again, thus losing all the advantages of the position, for at first there was only one battalion of the regiment of Moscow to defend the ravine.

The fate of an action frequently depends on being half an hour too late! Only one battalion of our regiment was engaged, and they left their knapsacks on the ground they had previously occupied. The French mistook these knapsacks for men lying down, and opened upon them a brisk fire of rifles. The commander of the No. 4 light battery, Colonel Kondratieff, a very active man, brought four guns to bear on these knapsacks in expectation of the French. It happened as he expected, for the French made a rush with the bayonet, and the four guns opened upon them and told heavily.

In the centre, while we were retreating, the regiment of Vladimir advanced to the support of those already engaged. It deployed into columns of battalions, and charged with the bayonet without any assistance from artillery, though there were still two batteries in reserve that had not fired a shot. It was received with great firmness by the English troops, and after a fearful struggle, in which it lost half its men, forced to retire in confusion. This proves that our generals had a very poor notion of military tactics, for to send a regiment to the charge without previously having weakened the enemy by artillery is contrary to all rule.

Prince Menschikoff showed a great deal of personal courage; four officers of his suite were killed near him by the fire from the fleet while he remained unmoved. But for a commander-in-chief courage is not the only quality required; in fact, it is a part of his duty not to expose himself, unless absolutely necessary, to the enemy's fire.

We remained on the hill a short time, above the position the army had previously occupied, when the major commanding the battalion decided that we must retreat. Skirmishers were thrown out while we went to the right-about and retired thirty yards, when we again came to a halt for five minutes, only to see that our army was utterly routed and beaten out of an almost unassailable position. The retreat then began in earnest; a few minutes afterwards we became exposed to a cross fire from the English and French batteries, and on all sides the men cried out "To the right!" "To the left!" to avoid the shot, and in one place they broke into a run. We had the greatest difficulty to keep our men in order. At one time I was obliged to threaten to cut down the first man who should break out of the ranks, and was unfortunately obliged to keep my word with one man.

It must, however, be said that the men of the 6th corps were all young soldiers, as this corps has always served as a depôt for the four first corps, and frequently for the 5th and 7th corps. Thus, after the campaign in Hungary, we sent to the number of sixty men per company to fill up the losses of the 2nd corps; sixty men per company will amount to 11,520 men, which were made up to us with recruits. In our regiment there were men who did not know how to load their firelocks; and when a man does not know how to use his arms, of course he will not have much confidence in himself when he hears shot, shell, and rifle-balls about his ears. In disorder we began our retreat, but whither no one knew. Prince Menschikoff rode past our battalion while we were under the fire of the artillery, and the men crying out "To the right!" "Left!" or "Take care!"

The prince said, as if to himself, "It's a disgrace for a Russian soldier to retreat."

Captain G——, who was near him at the time, and overheard these words spoken by the prince, answered in a loud tone, beginning with an oath, "If you had ordered us to stand, we should have stood our ground!" This officer was hardly sober, or he would not have dared to address the prince in such language, but under existing circumstances no notice was ever taken of it.

We retreated in disorder across the valley that divides the heights of the Alma from those of the Katcha, and on the latter heights we by some strange accident halted and formed into order of battle. I here saw the enemy's cavalry descend into the valley, and cut off retreating stragglers, for the most part wounded men. We remained on the second line of heights about ten minutes in fear and trembling, as we expected the enemy would have followed, and we knew that our only safety was in showing a bold front while the greater part of the army continued to retreat in disorder. We then continued our retreat. Here most of us began to draw our breath more freely, and to thank Heaven we were safe for that day at least, for we could no longer hear the balls whistling about our ears.

Here I asked the commander of the battalion whither we were going—I was ashamed to ask whither we were retreating, or rather running, for such it was. But the major did not know; he had no orders where to go. The colonel came up to our battalion, and inquired how many men we had lost.

"Twenty rank and file and one officer wounded."

This officer had left a bride in Moscow, promising to return to her after the first battle; his wound enabled him to keep his word. General Kiriakoff rode past us shortly afterwards, and ordered us to keep better order, saying that the officers were not looking to their men. Prince Gortchakoff soon after passed us looking for Menschikoff, who was nowhere to be found.

As I marched in my place with the men, I could not help overhearing the following conversation between two men of my own company:—"Yes!" says the first, "during the fight we saw nothing of these great folks, but now they are as thick as imps with their shouting 'Silence! keep step!' While we were fighting he was walking about, but now he has mounted his *fedoura* to swagger and shout at us!" (this was meant for the major).

The second said, "You are always grumbling, just like a Pole; you are enough to anger Providence, whom we ought to thank for our lives."

"It's all the same to you," says the first, "provided you are not flogged."

Unfortunately I could not listen to the remainder of this conversation; as you can never get a straightforward answer from a soldier about his officers, it is only by accidents like these that you can arrive at a knowledge of what they really think. One of my old schoolfellows came up with me at this moment. He was lieutenant in the regiment of Kazan.

After mutual congratulations that we were both unhurt, I asked him how his regiment had behaved. "Pretty well, considering we have not more than 800 men left out of 2500, our strength this morning. We have also lost a great many officers."

"Well, tell me how the English fought."

"Hush! the major is just behind us," answered he; "I shall see you again, and then I'll tell you all about it."

With this he rode off to his regiment.

The officers all marched slowly along, congratulating each other upon their escapes and trying to find some liquid to refresh themselves, as we were all frightfully tired, and nobody knew our destination. Some said we were to halt on the Katcha, where we should fight another battle. At this I could not help asking with what troops the battle was to be fought? Others said we were to march to Bakchi Sarai, others that we were to hold the Belbek, and some said we were to go to Sevastopol. We all stared at each other, and wondered where we should find ourselves at last; that Providence would lead us was our only hope, as we were like a flock of lost sheep without a shepherd. It was extremely fortunate for us that the Allies were not strong in cavalry, or not more than 15,000 would have ever reached Sevastopol. Horse artillery would have been very effective while we were crossing the Katcha at the village of Aranchi, where the greatest confusion reigned.

At this time all were crowding together over the river at a ford—there were commissariat wagons, artillery wagons, with wounded artillery, infantry, &c, in one mass of confusion. All these had to retire through a narrow pass surrounded on all sides by high mountains, from which had a shot or shell been thrown from time to time, it would have completed the disorganization, for none would have thought of resisting, so great was the demoralization of the men. After the passage of the ford, the confusion became, if possible, still greater, and all attempts to obtain some degree of order were useless; to increase all this, the evening now began to close upon us. Everybody seemed to have lost the faculties of thinking and acting; nobody mentioned the enemy or the defeat we had suffered; from the surprise which that occasioned our commanders could not recover; so we all hurried on, but no one knew whither! Our battalion, after crossing the Katcha, kept a southerly direction till it became quite dark; the men were so tired that they could hardly drag one leg before the other, when a Cossack galloped past us and said we were to go to the Katcha.

"Which is the way?" asked the major.

"Straight forward," cried the Cossack, as he galloped on to repeat the order to others. Straight forward! before us were hills, cliffs, and woods, with only a small path that led Heaven knows whither. Before proceeding farther, I begged the commander of our battalion to allow the men to rest a little. We got our battalion together, and discovered that two companies were missing—a sergeant, Ojogin, is sent back to shout, and try to make them hear or find them; but the poor fellow, tired and hungry, after running to and fro, could find no one. We discovered that we were alone in the hills, and knew not in what direction the rest of the army had retreated. A short distance in front of us I heard a groan as of someone in pain. I went to see what it was, and found a soldier who had been wounded by a ball in the leg above the knee; he told me he had been taken to the field-hospital and had his leg bandaged, when the surgeon told him to go to Sevastopol, a distance of about thirty versts, or twenty miles!

At first, he said, he trudged along pretty well, but from the exertion of walking the blood flowed freely from his wound, and saturated the bandage, which began to slip down, while the ball caused him great pain in walking; at last he was obliged to sit down to rest, and, wishing to rebandage his leg, he had taken off the ligature, when the blood, heated by his walk, flowed from the wound faster than ever, so that he could not stop it or help himself. There he lay, poor fellow! on the bare ground, alone in the field at night, without a creature to render him assistance, or by his society to lighten the difficulties of the road. The sight of this poor wounded man caused me to reflect that he had fought and done his duty, suffering in a cause the merits of which he knew nothing, and now wounded and helpless he could neither obtain assistance nor consolation.

It is surprising how little care is taken of a Russian soldier! I regretted extremely that I could not help him myself, but we had neither stretchers nor wagons with us; on appealing, however, to the men, some of them, tired as they were, agreed to take this unfortunate man with them. Major Iliashevitch objected to this, saying we had troubles enough of our own without adding to them by the charge of wounded men. We afterwards saw numbers of these unhappy wretches abandoned to their fate, and we could not have taken them all. There were wagons with every regiment, but these wagons on four wheels without springs are not perhaps the best means for transporting sick and wounded men. Even a healthy man who is unused to this mode of conveyance will feel very much shaken after travelling ten miles over a rough country road. The greater part of these wagons were used for the conveyance of wounded officers; and for officers who were not wounded but of delicate or nervous constitutions, so that a very small proportion of the wounded soldiers were able to ride in the vehicles provided for them.

After resting for some time, the major sent Lieutenant P——— on his horse, to try if he could find any men. He returned in about half an hour, and said he had seen nobody, but that to the left he had heard a rumbling noise as of wagons or artillery on the march. It was then resolved that we should move in the direction of the sound. We accordingly went by the way pointed out to us, and after some time we began to listen for the sounds spoken of but nothing was to be heard in that direction. Again we halted to call a council of war of all the officers left with the remains of the battalion. Our commanding officer put the question to us all,—"What are we to do?"

We were fairly alone in a country quite unknown to any of us; the darkness was so great that at a very short distance we could distinguish no object. To add to this, we were all completely tired out. Some proposed to turn to the left in order to get to Sevastopol. Others again said we must go to the right and not to the left for that purpose. In fact, we were completely lost, and might, for aught we knew to the contrary, be standing on the edge of a precipice. Some of our officers suggested that we had better remain on the spot till daylight and then go to Sevastopol.

"Yes," said the major, "and be made prisoners by the Englishmen in the morning"

At last he consented to remain, taking into consideration that we all required rest, though he then went himself in search of somebody who might be able to direct him. In a ravine not far from us he found the remains of the regiment of Moscow, not more than 300 men and six officers out of the four battalions; they were in the same unfortunate position that we were, not knowing where they were or which way to go.

Here a Cossack patrol came up with us, and gave us the order to go to the river Katcha as the general rendezvous of the army: he said he was sent to look for those who had lost their way, but he did not know which way led to the Katcha. Our position, therefore, was no better than before. The major again inquired of us if we knew the road to the Katcha, but without any result: he then turned to the men to know if any of them knew the road; a man from my company said he thought he could find it, as he had been sent from Sevastopol with prisoners to the cavalry, which was encamped on the Katcha, before the descent of the Allies. The major at this told the man to lead us there as quickly as possible.

We arrived, with the remnant of the regiment of Moscow, at

midnight, after a march of about an hour and a half. Major Ilia-shevitch wished me to look for the two lost companies of our battalion, but they were not to be heard of. On the banks of the river there were cavalry, artillery, and infantry, but no tidings of our lost sheep. Here I had the good fortune to find my servant, and was able to get some warm tea, for since the morning we had had nothing to eat or drink, as it was impossible to think of that during the battle and our wandering retreat. I was much surprised that we had few stragglers from our battalion, for I was very tired myself, having been twenty hours on my feet, and great was my joy to be able to ride to Sevastopol, as my servant had with him my horse as well as the tea and *somavar*.

After a rest of two hours we again began to retreat towards the town. During this halt I saw numbers of wounded who had bandaged their own wounds. On the road from the Katcha to the north side of Sevastopol we passed numbers of these unfortunate men, who cried out to us for help we could not give them. Some asked for water to quench their intolerable thirst, while others begged hard to be put at once out of their agony by a speedy death. These sights and sounds had a very visible effect upon the morale of the men, as they saw how little care was taken of them when they most required it. They exclaimed amongst themselves, while passing through these horrors, "Happy is he whom a merciful Providence permits to die on the field of battle!"

The colonel of our regiment rode alone in a small phaeton with a pair of fine horses! The men made their own reflections on this, saying, "See, at his own expense, but with our money, he has bought himself a carriage, but he does not think of helping the poor wounded soldiers who are lying about by the roadside, although a ride to the hospital would save their lives."

The sergeant went up to the man who said this, asking him how he dared to reason in that manner, giving weight to his observation by a blow or two in the face; the poor fellow tried to murmur out an excuse.

"So you are impudent, you rascal!" accompanied by more

blows from the sergeant. "Silence!" The poor soldier was obliged to digest both the blows and remarks of his superior.

This is the way the men are treated in the Russian army! I could not interfere, as this took place between men of another company, and on my remonstrating with the captain of that company he simply remarked, "I can't help it! it is the only way to treat such brutes!"

On our arrival at the north side of Sevastopol all the troops, except our regiment, crossed the harbour to the field of Kulikoff, to the south-west of the town. Our regiment took up the old encampment (see Chap. 1.), with No. 4 Light Battery, about 4 a.m. During the last march from the Katcha we had a good many stragglers, who kept coming in all the morning.

This was not at all extraordinary, for the men had been on their legs twenty-four hours, and had to carry their knapsacks, &c, which, without the firelock, amount to about 60 lbs. We now learnt that the regiment had lost 110 men killed and wounded and six officers. The cause of this slight loss was that only one of our battalions (the 4th) was engaged, and that only for a short time, with the French, while we only retreated in perfect order, as the Russian accounts say. The entire loss on the side of the Russians, according to the returns, was 1762 killed, 2315 wounded, and 405 contused, making a total of 4482 *hors de combat*. In the number of killed were forty-five officers, and among the wounded four generals. I have no means of verifying this statement, but as it is official it must be true! as they say in Russia. This was, at least, the account sent to the Emperor. The generals wounded were the commander of the 16th division, Lieutenant-General Kvitzinsky; the Brigadier-Generals of the 16th division, General Shchelkanoff, and of the 2nd brigade 17th division, General Goginoff; and the colonel of the regiment of Moscow, Major-General Kourtianoff; besides which there were 96 officers wounded.

If I might venture to give my opinion on the battle of the Alma, I should say that the Russians were beaten from the following causes—first, the troops were badly disposed upon the position; secondly, during the action nobody gave any directions what to do, and every one acted as he thought fit; the battalions of reserve began to retreat without any orders; our battalion also began to retire, following the example of the reserves. During the five hours that the battle went on we neither saw nor heard of our general of division, or brigadier, or colonel: we did not during the whole time receive any orders from them either to advance or to retire; and when we retired, nobody knew whether we ought to go to the right or left. In the centre of the line it was the same; and if the men fought, it was solely on the responsibility of the colonels of regiments, but certainly not from any orders of Prince Gortchakoff I.; for who would have thought of sending a regiment to the charge without its being supported by artillery, when there were plenty of guns in reserve? Where there was some degree of order was on the left flank, where Prince Menschikoff was in person; but it was difficult for him to stop the advance of the French troops, as he could not get up his reserves before they had crowned the heights.

The position occupied by each battalion and battery before the action began is accurately marked out on the plan that accompanies this chapter. Those battalions and batteries that were moved to the front during the action, and the direction they took, are marked by dotted lines. The retreat took place, as I said above, without any order, and every battalion moved when and where its commander thought advisable. After passing the valley, some of the battalions halted and formed into order of battle from a sort of instinct (this movement is also indicated on the plan); while some of the regiments formed a confused mass of columns of all their four battalions together—this was especially the case with those regiments that suffered most. With such confusion among the heads of the Russian army it is not surprising that the battle was lost; but a more ample proof of this will be seen in the 6th chapter, where a large army with a numerous artillery surprised a small body of Englishmen at Inkerman with every prospect of success, but were beaten off through the blunders of the commanders.

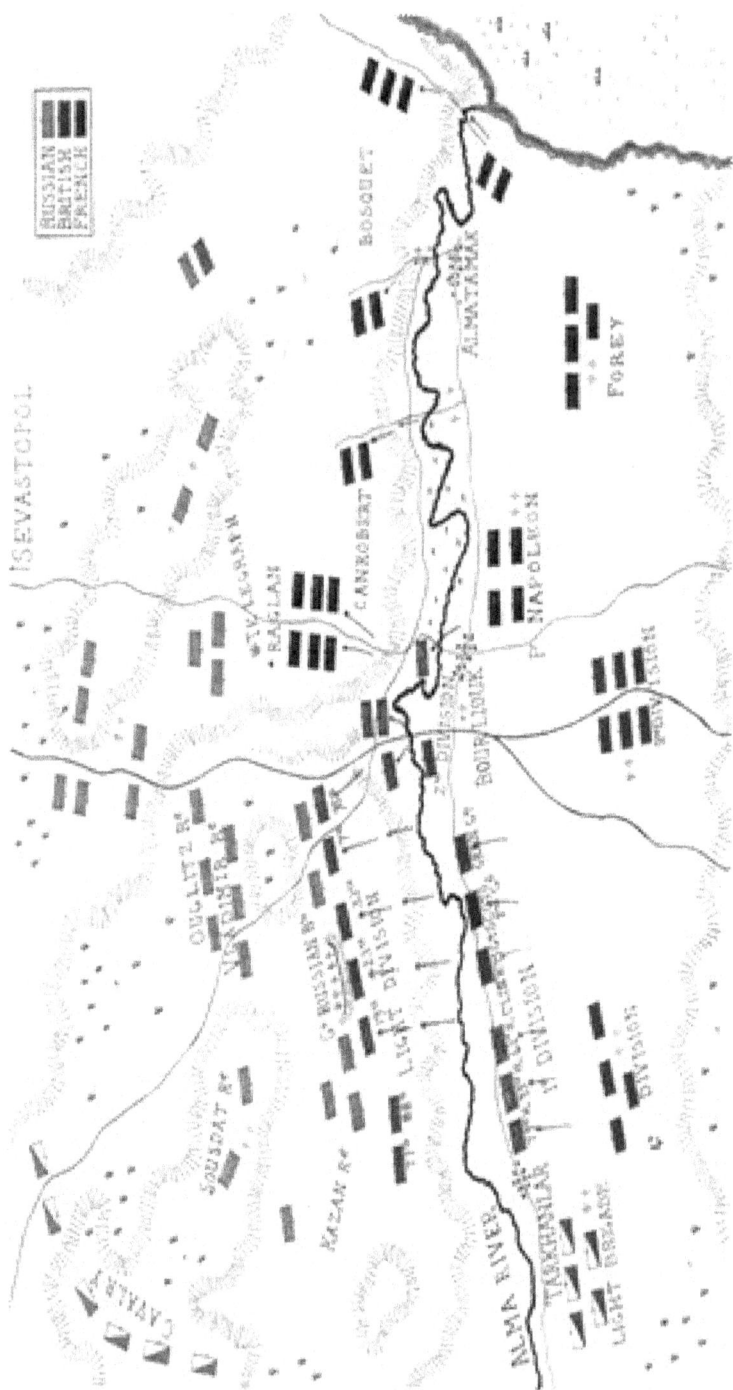

BATTLE OF ALMA

CHAPTER 4

The Defence of the City

On the morning of the 21st, as I was enjoying a profound sleep after the fatigues of the day before, a soldier of my company awoke me, saying that the sergeant had told him to inform me that the regiment was ordered to move.

"Where are we to go?" I asked.

"I don't know," said he.

It is scarcely to be conceived with what unwillingness I left my bed that morning—the bed consisted of the bare ground, with a soldier's knapsack for a pillow, and my grey great-coat for a covering. All our baggage was in store at the barracks of Sevastopol, so that I could get no better bed. There was no help for it. I was obliged to get up and arrange my toilette, which did not take long, as I slept in my clothes. I then joined the regiment, which had left the encampment and was already on the hills, about three *versts* from Outchkouevka, towards the harbour. Working parties were told off from each company to strike the tents, which had been left standing when we moved towards the Alma. No. 4 Light Battery of our brigade joined us. This battery suffered much at the Alma, where it was placed near the telegraph bearing on the French and the steamers, and lost more than half the men and a great many horses.

As they came up to our position, the commander of this battery, Colonel Kondratieff, shouted, "What can I do here, since I have few men and horses, and my gun-carriages are so much knocked about that they hardly hold together? I can be of no use."

Now it was to be seen how much the Russian army had lost in morale. From the Prince downwards not one knew what to do; they were all at their wits' ends. Nobody ventured to speak of the day before. The soldiers had lost their spirits, and they moved without any energy. I think they one and all would have willingly deserted to the enemy, if they had thought it possible. No other conversation was carried on but as to where they should hide their little property. While we were here I met Captain S——, who had boasted of his prowess while on the road to the Crimea. He was considered a literary man in the regiment, and might be taken for a clever fellow after half-an-hour's small talk; he was known as the Fly of Sosnoosk, the name under which he wrote, taken from the village he had been quartered in.

"What does the Fly of Sosnoosk say of the events of yesterday?" I asked of him.

"I intend to describe the battle, and show how I exposed my breast in defence of my country!" answered he.

"Oh, yes!" said I, "you certainly exposed your breast; but you will not mention how you ran away, I suppose!"

"Go to," said he, "there is no use in talking about these things!" and he went up to the major commanding the battalion.

Everybody tried to forget what had taken place, and seemed to be overcome by a kind of mortal fear. The men spoke in a low tone of their comrades killed and wounded, and in some cases criticised their officers' conduct the day before. A veteran, who had seen thirty years' service, said that he had seen a great many fields of battle, but he never saw such disorder as on the Alma, nor had he ever seen such commanding officers before in an action. "The fence is good, but the posts are not sound, and the whole fence fails," was his simple but expressive figure. The remark struck me as particularly à propos, and I could not resist ordering the man to be given a glass of vodka. I cautioned him however to be more careful, as another might overhear him who would reward him in another way.

"Ah, sir, I am now old! What can they do to me?"

"Take care; your age may not be respected by everyone; remember the Russian proverb!"

At 9 a.m. Prince Menschikoff rode up to us, looking very gloomy and cross, and asked for the colonel, who had not yet made his appearance, being, as I suppose, still fast asleep. Colonel Kondratieff reported to the prince the state of his battery, and the impossibility of his being effective in case of necessity. The prince ordered the battery to be transported across the harbour, and our regiment to take up a position on the heights at the mouth of the Belbek; when at eleven o'clock we formed in columns of companies without any artillery or support, for the purpose, as we supposed, of opposing the whole allied army. Four battalions against an army that had beaten forty-four battalions on a strong position!

I could not understand why our regiment was left there alone, unless it was because we had done so much at the Alma, where we were among the first to retreat without having fired a shot. Besides the prince was no friend of our colonel, who had talked so much of what he would do when before the enemy, but when the trial came was found wanting. It certainly is easy to say what one will do in case of being called to the field of action, while sitting at home; but the man who is most useful is he who shows himself in the field of battle to possess coolness to direct and courage to act.

About 5 p.m. a Cossack brought us the order to retire into the Severnaya fort. The men had eaten nothing all day, nor were we, their officers, in a better condition. Preparations were made for cooking the meal for the soldiers, who, however, were too tired to wait for their dinners, and lay down where they were in the square of the fort under the canopy of heaven. I and some more officers made our way to the rooms of a naval officer, begging him in the name of Heaven to give us food and lodging, which he did.

We all slept so soundly that I think if the fort had been bombarded that night we should have heard nothing of it. In the fort confusion reigned day and night; on each side trenches were being carried down to the sea on one side, and to the harbour in the direction of the barracks on the other. At each end of this trench batteries were erected, one near the sea, and the other on the heights behind the barracks. In the course of conversation that evening I inquired after Captains Volkhoff and Michno. "They have reported themselves sick," said Major G——, "but don't you know they are both related to the colonel? Volkhoff is his son, and Michno his son-in-law."

"Well, what has that to do with it?" asked I; "I can hardly understand you."

"I see you are a child in the service still," said he; "the son has reported himself wounded, and the son-in-law sick of a fever, and who dares to question the truth of their reports? If I were to report myself, a doctor would be sent immediately to examine and report upon the state of my health, while no notice is taken of them."

"But when," exclaimed I, "was Captain Volkhoff wounded, since I saw him in his tent last night, and he appeared quite well; besides, during the action he was near me all the time, and I saw that he took great care of himself, keeping behind his men, and when a round shot took off the arm of a drummer near him, and sent the drum into the air, Captain Volkhoff sprang from the place he was standing on, as if he had been bitten by a serpent!"

"When you have lived a little longer in the world," answered the veteran, "and seen more service, you will better be able to understand the meaning of being related to the colonel."

I was obliged to account for this by supposing that Captain Volkhoff was shamming. This the more surprised me as he was always boasting of defending his country against her invaders, and I thought he really was one of those who would lay down their lives for their Tzar and fatherland; besides he was a very tall, well-built fellow, with an enormous moustache and a fine open countenance. His appearance was most prepossessing, and that with his boasting deceived me. Captain Volkhoff reported himself wounded when he was untouched, and went into Sevastopol, and we heard no more of the son of the colonel. Among the officers of our regiment there were about twenty who did nothing but look to their own interest. When rewards were to be distributed they were the first to obtain them, or, if any one was to be distinguished, it was sure to fall to the lot of one of these; while if any officers who tried to do their utmost were remarked, it was said that they only did their duty as every man ought to do.

At 6 a.m. on the 22nd our 1st and 2nd battalions were ordered upon fatigue duty in the Severnaya fort; the sailors of the fleet had been at work there for some time before. Great efforts were made to complete this fort. More guns were added to those already mounted. Our 3rd and 4th battalions were sent to our old encampment, in order to transport it into the fort, with all the property of the regiment: every one hurried, trying to finish his work, as we were expecting the enemy upon us every hour. As there are no wells in Fort Severnaya, the convicts were employed in transporting iron tanks into the citadel, and filling them with water.

The commandant of Fort Severnaya, Major-General Pavlovsky, collected us about 10 a.m., and informed us that our regiment, with one equipage of sailors and the four depot battalions of the 13th division, formed the garrison of Fort Severnaya. He then pointed out to us where we were to place our men in case of an attack, and in what case-mates we were to take refuge in case of a cannonade, and other arrangements made for the reception of the enemy. Should we be unable to hold Fort Severnaya, we were to retreat by the subterranean passage that leads to the Kourin Balka. The officer in command of the sappers received orders at the same time to prepare four fougasses opposite the eastern face of the fort. After all these arrangements were made, I asked leave to go into the town about 12 a.m., as I could find nothing to eat within the fort.

I availed myself of this opportunity to ascertain what had happened in the town between the 13th and 22nd of September, The chief of the staff of the Black Sea fleet, Admiral Korniloff, worked hard and successfully at the defences of the south side of the harbour: the works were carried on day and night up to the 20th; everybody waited with anxiety the result of the first meeting with the enemy, when it was known at 8 p.m. of that day that the army had been defeated on the Alma, and was flying towards Sevastopol. It would be impossible to call the retrograde movement of the Russian army from the Alma else than a flight, for the disorder and confusion that reigned were complete.

The chiefs of the army are to be blamed for not having made any arrangements for taking proper care of the wounded. This proves that either the prince never expected an invasion of the Crimea, or that, foreseeing the event, he was guilty of neglect in not establishing proper hospitals for the wounded that might have been expected to result from the struggle. During the night of the 20th-21st these unfortunate men arrived in the town, for the most part with their wounds undressed. Few of them were lucky enough to ride, but dragged their mutilated limbs in the greatest agony on foot. To the honour of the Russian soldiers be it said that many tore up their shirts for the purpose of bandaging the wounds of their comrades, neglected and left to their fate from the want of proper arrangements for their accommodation.

The next day these poor remnants of humanity continued to arrive. The prince reached the town about 11 o'clock on the night of the 20th, and then it began to become generally known that the army was defeated. Besides, the battalions of sailors, who were among the first to arrive, were sent to their homes, and they were not long in spreading the news of the discomfiture. At midnight the prince called a council of war, consisting of all the admirals and many of the naval officers in the town. They looked at each other in the greatest consternation; what had best be done was asked on all sides. The enemy was expected before the town by daylight, when he would open a vigorous bombardment. What could be done?

Many were the plans of defence proposed. Admiral Korniloff

advised that six vessels should be moored across the mouth of the harbour from Fort Constantine to Fort Alexander; that on the approach of the allied fleets each should fire a broadside and then be sunk at their anchors, while the crews could escape to the shore in their boats. These ships would form an impassable barrier to the enemy's fleet. This plan was adopted almost unanimously, but Prince Menschikoff resolved to sink the ships at once.

That night orders were given that the crews of the following ships should transport all their effects to the shore:—the *Tree Sviatitel*, i.e., *Three Bishops*, three-decker; the *Safaïl* and *Uriel*; two-deckers, with the frigates *Varna* and *Med*, and one old two-decker, the *Bachmout*, which was before placed in Careening Bay to be used as a battery. After having placed their property in safety, the crews of these six ships returned to them, and in the morning these sacrifices to the defence of the town were at their stations.

On the morning of the 21st a perfect chaos reigned throughout the town; drunken sailors wandered riotously about the streets, and in some instances shouted that Menschikoff had sold the place to the English, and that he had purposely been beaten at the Alma, where he had caused confusion by giving no directions during the battle; many similar ideas were current among the drunken populace and sailors. The prince did not show himself about the town. Korniloff alone endeavoured to restore order and confidence among the inhabitants, and his exertions for the defence are worthy of the highest praise.

All the cellars for the sale of liquor were ordered to be closed, as well as all the inns and hotels or other places where spirituous liquors could be obtained; but this appeared to have had little or no effect in restraining the populace from drunkenness, when the order was given to destroy all the spirits or wines that could be found on the premises of those entitled to sell them. I went into an hotel to get some dinner, when I was told I could have nothing, as the police had ordered them not to sell anything. The only hotel in the town that was allowed open was that of one Schneider, in Ekatherine Street, where officers alone were allowed to enter. Soldiers, sailors, convicts, and the inhabitants of the town were all forced to work at its defences. The prince seemed lost, and not to know what to do. He appeared to have lost all courage and energy. Some time before this two fire-ships had been prepared for the purpose of burning the enemy's fleet, should that come near the town, but these were now sunk at the head of the harbour, near the Inkerman Bridge.

During the night of the 21st-22nd, the six ships above-mentioned were sunk with all their armament and stores for three months, with the exception of the *Bachmout*. The loss, without counting the ships themselves, must have been very great. The *Tree Sviatitel* would not sink after being scuttled; so about 8 a.m. of the 22nd, the steamer *Vladimir* fired three shots into her from a very short range; but still she floated on the waters.

At this time a man belonging to the *Vladimir* went up to his captain and asked if he might go to the doomed ship, and take out of her a miraculous image that had been given by the bishop of Odessa when the ship was launched, as, said the man, that is the cause of her not sinking. The captain with a smile granted his request, and he returned triumphantly with the prize, which he showed his captain, exclaiming, "How could you expect a thing so holy to sink!" Two more shots sent the vessel to the bottom. This little circumstance will serve to show the amount of fanaticism that exists among the lower orders in Russia, which is exploited by the government. This man was firmly convinced that the image could and would never sink!

After the sinking of these ships, there remained the following:— three-deckers, the *Twelve Apostles, Paris*, the *Empress Maria*, and *Constantine*; two-deckers, *Sviatoslav, Gavriel, Chrabri, Chesma*, and *Yagoodiel*; frigates, *Koolevchi, Kogal, Kovarna*, and *Koulevchi*; steamers, *Vladimir*, 12 guns, *Gromonosetz*, 6 guns, *Chersoness*, 8 guns, *Imberus*, 4 guns, *Bessarabia*, 6 guns, *Danube*, 6 guns, *Odessa*, 4 guns, *Turk*, and *Severnaya Zvezda,* two small tugs, with an Egyptian that was taken before the battle of Sinope. Besides these there were six corvettes and ten brigs and schooners.

In the town the people were as busy as ants, working day and night at the defences. The greater number of the wives and families of the naval officers were at this time in the town. As it was not known where the enemy might be expected, they were afraid to retire to Simpheropol. In fact, all seemed to be seized with a kind of panic. Korniloff appeared to have a power of multiplying himself, for he was everywhere, encouraging those at work, and promising large rewards to all, if they could only keep the town. He consequently was decidedly popular, while all were discontented with Menschikoff and the other commanders. Even the infantry grumbled at the way the prince had acted, but all this discontent was kept down, as no one dared to give open expression to his opinions or feelings.

In the evening I returned to Fort Severnaya, where, as I said before, my regiment was stationed. I could not, however, find anywhere to sleep, so was obliged to pass the night in the square of the fort under the canopy of heaven.

The next morning, the 23rd, on getting up I found that my company was already at work. In the course of conversation I learned that the colonel had sent four men to look for his relatives, mentioned above, when they were both found hiding in the Karabelnaya suburb and brought back to the regiment, where they were allowed to go unpunished. They did not appear at all ashamed of having shirked their duty in the service of their country, while that country and its faith were in danger and required their services. These men were both Russians! What can the men say when they see their officers show in this way the white feather?

While in the town, the day before, I had met a man of our regiment, and, knowing it was against orders for him to cross the harbour, I asked him what he came for.

"I am looking," said he, " for the captain; the sergeant-major sent me."

"Is he ill, or what?"

"Yes, sir," said he; "they say that his nobility does not like the nuts we get from the enemy!"

It cannot be expected that the men should have respect for or confidence in such officers as these, who never show them an example in a moment of danger. This is the great misfortune of the Russian army.

About two o'clock we moved out of the fort on to the heights at the mouth of the Belbek, where we took up our position, as on the 21st, in columns of companies. Along the shore a steamer belonging to the allied fleet was cruising, and, without doubt, watching our movements. The regiment of Borodino, 1st Regiment of our brigade; the regiment of Moscow, 1st regiment of the 1st brigade of our division, with two field batteries and one regiment of Hussars; the regiment of Leuchtenberg of the 2nd brigade of the 6th cavalry division, having crossed the Inkerman bridge, halted in the wood to our right.

We now learned that the general of our division had asked the prince to allow him, with these troops, to make a flank movement upon the enemy; and in case his retreat should be cut off from Sevastopol he was to retreat to Simpheropol, but if the enemy pressed after him he was to retreat to Perecop. I could not help fancying that in this movement he had his eye upon Moscow, the pleasures of which place he had left with regret, and Perecop was nearer than Sevastopol. At 5 p.m. General Kiriakoff rode tip to us and ordered our regiment to move to the right, towards the post-station at the bridge of Belbek. The moment we began to march the steamer stopped and evidently watched our movements. I could not help risking the remark to the colonel, that success was impossible, as we were still observed by the steamer.

He simply answered, "That's not your affair."

I thought, "Well, God forgive them! They know not what they do!"

As we disappeared into the wood the steamer moved off, as I naturally supposed, to give information of the fact. We then, *i.e.* our regiment, formed on the left-hand side of the road leading to the post-station, with the regiment of Moscow in our rear; while on the other, or right-hand side of the road, was the regiment of Borodino with the cavalry, and on the road itself was the artillery. The men were allowed to descend to the river to get water, and they were just going to water the artillery and cavalry horses when the general shouted out for us all to take our places in the ranks, and we retired up the hill at a good pace, having stood about a quarter of an hour.

"What is the matter?" asked I of one of the general's *aides-de-camp*, who was riding by.

"Look there, on the hill is the enemy's cavalry!" said he.

"Yes," I remarked; "if things are not arranged a little better, we shall soon all be prisoners in the hands of the enemy."

Our regiment received orders to go into the wood to the right, and to remain till ordered to move. Here, then, we began to make our little arrangements for sleeping.

This is another of the proofs of the incapacity of our general. He wished to make a flank movement while within sight of the enemy, and actually showed them what he intended to do and where to go. If I might venture to offer an opinion, I should think our regiment ought to have been left till night; then to have lighted fires, which could have been kept up by a few Cossacks, who would also have made a noise, and then it would not have been extraordinary if the Allies had supposed us there. In the meantime we could have moved towards the left flank of the opposing army, and at daylight attacked; for a surprise as intended it would be necessary to have muffled the gun-wheels, &c., and the mouths of the horses to prevent neighing.

When a movement of this kind is well arranged it generally succeeds from the unexpectedness of the attack. But our general was obliged to send to the prince to say that he wanted to know what to do, as he had failed in his undertaking, because he was discovered—a very natural result when he begins his movement under the very nose of a cruiser who is watching him, The prince could only send one order—"For us to retire."

About 1 a.m. the troops began to retire towards the Inkerman Bridge. That day I was the orderly officer of the regiment, consequently could not sleep as the others. I went to examine our outposts, as we were now afraid of being surprised and attacked in our turn. On returning to the regiment I heard a great noise in the rear, and sent a non-commissioned officer to learn the cause. The man ran back, and told me that all the other troops were retiring. I could not understand this at all, as we had had no orders, so I went myself and found the others already moving, while we were quite forgotten. I returned and woke the colonel, whom I found asleep under a tree on some dry leaves, and informed him that the rest of our column was retreating.

At first he would not believe me, and exclaimed, "Why were we not informed of this movement?"

"I cannot say, your Excellency," said I, "but I have been myself and seen that they are all retiring."

The colonel then descended himself to the road, and found nobody there—they were all gone. He ordered the 4th battalion to move, after which the rest of the regiment followed.

We crossed the river Chernaya by the Inkerman Bridge, leaving four guns opposite to it with the 4th battalion of our regiment, while the other three battalions moved higher up the heights into the brushwood, of which there are now no traces.

About 4 o'clock on the morning of the 24th we took up our position. The fog was very dense, and the cold seemed to penetrate to our very bones. The number of sick was very great; from my company alone I sent ten men to the hospital; nor was this at all extraordinary, considering that we had been nearly twenty-four hours without any food, and had undergone great exertions. About noon I went up to the top of the hill opposite the Inkerman Bridge, and saw the Cossacks busily employed burning the hay that had been stacked near our old encampment. This is a part of Russian tactics, that nothing useful should be left for the use of the enemy, though they sometimes suffer themselves from this over-caution.

At 4 p.m. the 3rd battalion of our regiment was ordered to relieve the 4th, under the orders of a colonel whose name I have forgotten, and to whom the defence of the bridge was committed, with four field-guns and four siege-guns of a large calibre.

At the same time the rest of the regiment received orders to prepare for moving, but whither, no one knew, not even the colonel. The whole of our regimental transport was in the town, and the men were allowed to take as much black biscuit as they chose before marching; but few of them took much, as they calculated they would have to carry it on their own backs.

At 5 p.m. we began to move, passed the windmill on the Woronzow road, and began to descend towards the river Chernaya. It then began to be rumoured that we had a Greek for a guide, who would conduct us to the flank, and even to the rear of the enemy, and that at daybreak we were to attack. I must say I thought the plan a good one, and likely to be successful, but of the details of course I knew nothing. The men, however, took heart, and marched gaily along.

On reaching the left bank of the river we discovered that the other troops had already crossed, and that we were the last; we passed the river at the ford at Chorgoun, where our rapid march began to tell upon the strength of the men, for many fell out quite knocked up. I was on foot all the time myself, and felt excessively fatigued when we began the ascent up to Mackenzie's Farm. Here the road is narrow, with a precipice on one side; and, as the night was dark, several men fell over and were dashed to pieces. I saw two of these accidents; one of the victims was an excellent non-commissioned officer of the name of Ojoghin. This was not to be wondered at, as many of the men, from over-fatigue, appeared almost to sleep as they went, and one false step was enough to launch them into eternity. I heaved a sigh of contentment when we reached the summit of this steep hill, and found that the hussars had already lighted fires for us. Captain L—— informed me that the fires had been lighted in order to deceive the enemy, while we were to advance and attack him at daybreak.

"Yes," I remarked; "but where will the men find strength to go any farther, since they are already knocked up with the march?"

On the heights we found the remains of the 16th division,

under the command of General Jobokritsky (the commander of the 16th division was taken prisoner at the Alma), a very energetic and able general. When we were ordered to halt I threw myself on the ground near one of the fires, and, having told the men to see that I did not set my clothes on fire, I slept more soundly than I ever did before, with a log of wood for my pillow. The Russian long grey coat is very good for a bivouac, except when it gets wet, and then the weight is intolerable. In about two hours, or half-past two in the morning, we were again ready to start; the 16th division had moved about an hour earlier.

It is very agreeable to be a man of high rank in the Russian army on these marches, since he can have his own carriage and horses, and when he is tired of sitting, he can stretch his legs at will. But to walk is no joke; on all sides the officers shouted keep up! Keep close! All marched till they were ready to drop, as they feared to fall into the hands of the enemy. The day began to break as we descended the heights of Mackenzie towards Otarkoi on the Belbek. The men were now completely beaten, and began to exclaim that they could go no farther. Some of them grumbled that the colonel was riding in his carriage, while they were all obliged to walk; many had thrown away their kits, and some were bold enough to abandon their knapsacks.

The biscuit with which some of them had loaded themselves at starting had been long since thrown away; numbers fell down from sheer exhaustion, and, I have no doubt, died where they fell. Where were the wagons and carts allowed for emergencies like these to carry the sick and tired soldiers? Most probably in the colonel's pockets, or perhaps invested in the purchase of the carriage and horses that carried him now. It is extremely profitable to be colonel of a Russian regiment, especially of the 6th Corps. If the question is asked, why is there no transport, the answer is sure to be "that the colonel is careful with the property of the regiment."

So it is with everything else. In war-time 240 horses are allowed as the transport for the regiment, but there are seldom more than half that number, and these are seldom used, as the colonel buys them out of a sum allowed him for that purpose. Besides the regimental transport there is generally a pair of horses, and sometimes more, in each company, bought with soldiers' money; these are driven about in all directions, as their loss is nothing to the colonel, but is felt by the captains of companies.

At 7 o'clock on the morning of the 25th we crossed the Belbek by a ford at Otarkoi and halted for an hour. Here we met some mountain guns, that had just returned from the Caucasus, which were going to Sevastopol to be placed in store. We again moved on till we came to a position, called by the Tatars Tazoba, where we found the 16th division, the 1st brigade of the 14th division, the cavalry, and—what was very refreshing to us—some vineyards and orchards. We halted here an hour and a half, and then continued our march to within four versts of Bakchi Sarai, and halted at a place called by the Tatars Izoba.

We had marched from five o'clock the evening before, till two o'clock in the afternoon, when we reached this position. At six o'clock in the evening we again moved back to Tazoba, to join the rest of the army under Prince Gortchakoff I. After the battle of the Alma, Menschikoff had given the command of the army to Gortchakoff I., and that of the town to Admiral Korniloff, who showed that he was worthy of the high confidence placed in him. Prince Menschikoff occupied a kind of neutral position, but remained with the staff of Prince Gortchakoff. This I know, as I saw Menschikoff at Tazoba while we were under the command of Gortchakoff I.

In the evening I was sent by the colonel to Colonel Vounsh, chief of the staff of the 6th corps, to ask if he had any vodka (a corn spirit erroneously called in public papers raki) for the men. He told me there was none. Here I learnt that the transport of the hussar regiment of Weimar, and the infantry regiment of Minsk, had been seized by the enemy's cavalry. The transport had been under a guard of two companies of the regiment of Minsk with an officer, who escaped with great difficulty to relate the disaster. He also spoke of the coolness of a non-commissioned officer of the hussars, who, with great presence of mind, broke open the regimental chest, and got out all the government money, which he brought with him to his regiment. He had not time to save the money of private individuals contained in the chest, which fell into the hands of the English, and, as I learnt afterwards, was returned by Lord Raglan, with that generosity which ever characterised his Lordship.

The ground occupied by our regiment was near the 16th division; that had been there for some hours, and consequently the ground was in such a state as to render all idea of lying down for the night hopeless. We had left our transport behind us on the march, and having learnt the fate of the transport of the regiments Weimar and Minsk, we were all on the *qui vive* to know what had become of ours. We were not very anxious about our money, but a little black biscuit would have been far more acceptable; we feared that the whole of the latter had fallen into the hands of the Allies; even the officers could get nothing. At last our men begged for something to eat of the 16th division, who took pity on their forlorn state.

On the morning of the next day, the 25th, our transport arrived, and was received in great glee by the men, as it gave them some prospect of a dinner; and the *shchi* (a kind of soup) made with fresh cabbage was delicious—perhaps our fasting had sharpened our appetites, and deadened our palates. At 3 p.m. we again moved to the position of Izoba on the river Katcha, where we were the day before. Soon after starting we heard firing at a distance; when the men, thinking they were pursued, were ready to run away, and kept looking round to see if the enemy made his appearance.

The position of Izoba is a very good one, situated on the right side of the river Katcha, which has precipitous banks, and is crossed by one bridge, over which passes the road to Bakchi Sarai, while at the distance from the river of about half a cannon-shot, there runs a range of small hills from which artillery might operate upon the river with effect. It would be impossible also to assail this position in flank; but if the Allies had once gained possession of Bakchi Sarai there would have been no difficulty in taking the great part of the army prisoners, as the men were too much demoralized to fight, and our communications with Russia would then have been cut off.

The chief defect, however, of this position was, that should we be forced to retire by an attack in front, the retreat must be to Bakchi Sarai, to which there existed only one road after the junction of the two roads from Sevastopol, that takes place before reaching the Katcha; by one of these two roads we had reached our present position, and on the other, that leads through the village of Belbek, was stationed the 16th division under General Jabokritzky as an advanced guard to the army. If we had been forced to retreat to Bakchi Sarai, which is, as it were, in a cauldron, entirely surrounded by high and commanding hills, we must have been destroyed. These movements of our army, which were directed by Prince Menschikoff, were both daring and desperate, and might have been disastrous, though, as events turned out, it proved successful to a certain extent. Of this anyone, who will take the trouble to follow our movements on the map, can easily judge for himself, knowing the forces we had at our disposal.

The troops in the town of Sevastopol at this time were the four battalions of reserve of the 13th division, that suffered considerably at the Alma, with the four depot battalions of the same division, and the 3rd battalion of our regiment, which we had left at the Inkerman Bridge, but which eventually retired into the town.

The army remained on the position of Izoba from the 25th September to the 1st October. I am not able to affirm whether Menschikoff was with the army the whole of this time, as I did not see him; but Prince Gortchakoff I. had the command. The soldiers were very glad of this rest, and visited the neighbouring villages daily. These villages they plundered to a fearful extent, so that it was not surprising that the Tatar inhabitants effected their escape on our approach, though they were obliged to abandon the greater part of their property to the spoilers. It was extraordinary to see the men, in their anxiety to obtain something, bring up to the camp the most useless and cumbersome articles, which they could never hope to transport. A lady, living on her estate near the village of Soula, was obliged to obtain a guard of soldiers to protect herself from being insulted, and her property from being plundered by the men who were fighting for her country and her faith.

On the day after our arrival the men began to complain that they were without biscuit, and on the captains of companies reporting the circumstance to the colonel, he replied, "I ordered the men to take provisions for four days—they must do as they can, now." It was very easy for him to talk in this way, but I think it not at all extraordinary that the men did not carry their provisions through such a tremendous march as we had performed. We were two days without biscuit or bread, till at last our colonel borrowed some from the regiment of Borodino. The fruits that we obtained here were the most delicious I think I ever ate, and were some compensation for the want of bread that we experienced.

The valleys of the Alma, Katcha, and Belbek were celebrated for their vineyards and orchards, which, thanks to the Russian soldiers, no longer exist. The most unbounded licence existed then in the Russian army, as the officers were afraid to curb the men in the field. An incident that serves as an illustration to this occurred while we were on the Katcha. One of my men, during the plundering of a village, insulted an old woman, who had remained to defend her property, and would not allow him to take it. This was brought to my notice, and I informed the commander of the battalion of it, and asked his permission to punish the man. He answered that as we were in the field any punishment inflicted might create an ill-feeling among the men that would eventually prove dangerous. What he meant by this will be seen in the account of the battle of Inkerman. I however insisted that if the men were to be treated thus there would be an end of all discipline, for they would soon find out that they were feared by their officers; while in a time of peace the soldiers are punished for the slightest offence, here the gravest must be overlooked because we are on campaign.

With such a system there will be no possibility of getting the men to obey, and they will do as they like. I at last carried my point upon the condition that I would take all the responsibility upon myself before the men, to which I consented, and had the man punished before the company. I also took advantage of the occasion to inform the company that I was determined to do my duty whether in the field or elsewhere, and that all evil-doers would receive their just award of punishment, as I did not fear their bullets. The discipline of the Russian army is very severe, and in some case it is carried to atrocity; but when the army takes the field there is a relaxation of all punishments, as the officers are anxious to conciliate the men by these means. This I never could practise—I would never inflict an undeserved punishment to please my own caprice, nor would I let off a man because I feared him. My idea always was, that the men ought to fear and respect, if not love, me, and from one of these motives obey me, but I never could conceive that I ought to fear them.

As our encampment was near Bakchi Sarai, I obtained permission to go for the day to that town. Here there were a great many soldiers and Tatars about the streets, along which, and very thickly, were posted the soldiers of the police, armed to the teeth. At these the Tatars looked with anything but a friendly glance, for these old inhabitants of the Crimea began to think that they were soon to be relieved from the yoke of their invaders. In this idea they were confirmed by what happened at Simpheropol.

On the 24th the mail for Sevastopol, on reaching the station at Duvaukoi, learnt that the allied armies were before it, so the man in charge of the mail-bags returned to Simpheropol in order to obtain assistance from the Governor-General Pestal, which he gave in the form of a guide and a guard. The Governor on this, thinking the danger imminent, ordered that all should leave the town with the greatest possible speed. The same order was repeated from the Government offices. The garrison battalion with the invalid command, that had lately retreated from Eupatoria, were ordered to evacuate the town and encamp. All the important personages, such as the commander of the gendarmes, the police master, &c, were directed to repair forthwith to the residence of the Governor.

The inhabitants of the town, who had the means, immediately made ready for the start, while their poorer neighbours were seen with their goods and chattels on their backs with the intention of pitching their tents in the fields. The Governor himself, accompanied by gendarmes, policemen, and all the officials, rode in great state through the streets, and out of the town, in the presence of large crowds of Tatars, who, dressed in gala costume, and on horseback, shouted in great glee,—"See, the *giaour* runs! Our deliverers are at hand!" Major Bronitzky, the late commandant at Eupatoria, took counsel with the commander of the garrison battalion, and they resolved to send information to Menschikoff of the events that had taken place at Simpheropol.

When Menschikoff heard of this he was beside himself with rage, and exclaimed, "How dared Pestal do all this without my orders? Command him from me to return to the town immediately, and not to stir till he has directions from me!"

It may be necessary to state that in Russia, during a war, the theatre of that war is under the orders of the commander-in-chief of the army, and of course all the other employés, whether civil or military, are bound to attend to his directions. Consequently General Pestal had no right to act upon his own responsibility. The consequences of this inconsiderate act were that it raised the hopes of the Tatar inhabitants of the Crimea, and some of the Greek and Armenian Christians fell victims to the outburst of the oppressed people, since the notice was so short that many were unable to leave the town with the Governor and military forces, and remained without any protection. The poorer classes asked for aid from the Governor, but such was his haste to leave the town that he had not time even to carry off all the Government property that was entrusted to him. The object of this extraordinary exodus was only to encamp around the town, and, when the order of Prince Menschikoff came to return, the Governor with his gendarmes, police, and employés, returned in triumph to his house. Shortly after this, Pestal was exchanged for Colonel Adlerberg, who became the Governor in his stead. The account of this affair I heard from one of the officers of our regiment, and from Greeks and Armenians who came to our camp with produce for sale.

At ten o'clock in the morning of the 1st of October we left our position on the Katcha and marched through Duvaukoi to the post-station of Belbek; when on the heights on the left bank of the river Belbek we halted for the night, with our front towards the sea. Here we learnt that the allied army was all before the south side of Sevastopol. We found too traces of the passage of an enemy through the country, for a large quantity of iron was strewed about; a convoy of that metal intended for Sevastopol having been seized here. There was also a large quantity of offal, most probably of the slaughtered oxen employed to transport the iron, strewed on the slopes of the hills, and by the sides of the road.

On the morning of the 2nd we formed into fighting order on the heights; hut the position was not one convenient for deploying, so the commander of our battalion and Captain Samarin asked of the men who marked the points who had placed them there.

"Colonel Zaletzki," answered the man. "There, that's another Pole! These fellows spoil everything, and through them we lose our battles!"

That is the view the Russians take of us, said yet we are obliged to serve, and it is a remarkable fact that a large proportion of the employments that require learned men are filled by Poles. We are always open to attacks in this way. After standing here about two hours we advanced, and as we reached the Severnaya Fort we met a great many wagons, carts, and carriages leaving the town with the inhabitants, for the most part women, who were escaping to Simpheropol, or into the interior of Russia. We descended to a wharf near Fort Michael, where a steamer embarked us and transported us to Grafskoi Pristan, near Fort

Nicholas.

Thence we marched up to the Place du Théâtre, where we remained in the open air. Here I met some of the officers of our 3rd battalion that had been left on the 24th of September at the Inkerman Bridge. They related that the enemy had made a reconnaissance at the bridge; but that all those who approached the dyke were fired at, which caused them to retire and to cross the heights of Mackenzie, and go on to Balaclava. Our 3rd battalion then retreated into the town, and took up a position near the Infantry Hospital, where it remained till our arrival, when it joined the regiment. The next day, 3rd, the 4th battalion of our regiment was placed in the ravine between the batteries: from this battalion, with sailors from the batteries, a portion of the men were sent out at night as advanced sentries.

Out of curiosity I crossed over to the Karabelnaya to see what had been done to the fortifications since we left on the 13th of September. From Krim Balka to Quarantine Bay a regular line of fortification had been established; and where there were not more than fifty guns at the time of the descent of the allies, there were now three hundred iron throats ready to vomit death upon those who might attempt the assault. All the sailors and soldiers worked day and night at the fortifications; besides, the inhabitants of the town were forced to labour in the defence of their homes. The very women were employed, and I remember one battery at which I saw them at work. This battery was not finished till after the opening of the bombardment, and was called the Women's battery. It is situated on the hill behind the theatre.

In the Karabelnaya, near Krim Balka, a battery was constructed that received the name of bastion No. 1. The battery was increased in size, and called bastion No. 2. These two bastions were connected by a trench and zigzags, while between them were four small houses, enclosed by a stone wall and the laboratory, that were used by the garrison. The laboratory was not then used, but rockets and other things were prepared elsewhere. Before the Malakhoff tower a semicircular earthwork had been erected, that was called with the tower the Malakhoff Bastion. The battery on the Bandory had been also increased and called the bastion No. 3., from which a short trench on the eastern side ran down towards the Karabelnaya ravine. These were the defences of the Karabelnaya suburb; to these guns were constantly being added day and night, so that it would be impossible to say what their numbers might be. In the town itself the battery was strengthened and enlarged, while several guns of large calibre were added to it; it received the name of bastion No. 4. The battery received the addition of a lunette on each flank; and before the tower a semicircular battery was constructed, while on the tower itself there were placed six guns, with the name of bastion No. 5. This bastion was connected originally with the bastion No. 4 by a low dry wall, which was now banked up with earth, and a trench made on the outside. In front of the store magazine that was in the loopholed wall, there was a semicircular work called the bastion No. 6. These were the additions that were made to the fortifications of the south side of the harbour from the middle of September to the beginning of October.

These works were all of earth, without any gabions to revet them, while the cheeks of the embrasures were simply clay moistened and plastered with a shovel, so that they were generally shaken down by the concussion after a few discharges from the guns in them; they were then again repaired with moistened clay and the shovel. This was the solidity of these works at first! At this time there were no batteries within the town, nor was the second line of defences begun. With great labour the town had been surrounded. At the head of the southern harbour was moored a two-decker, the *Yagondiel*, which was placed as near the head of the harbour as the depth of the water would allow.

The guns for the batteries were chiefly taken from the ships, though some were from the arsenal. All the gun-carriages were of naval construction, except in the sea batteries and forts. Few guns were left in Fort Nicholas. The streets of the town were crowded with guns, gun-carriages, shot, timber, &c, that were being continually conveyed to the batteries; all was noise, shouts, and confusion. From the batteries could be seen, here and there, the allied troops as they moved about their trenches, brought up guns or stores; the best view was from bastions Nos. 4 and 5.

Admiral Korniloff visited daily the works and encouraged the men to do their utmost. He said they must work hard now, but that it would soon be over, as success must and would crown their efforts. The garrison was increased daily by the arrival of new reinforcements: four battalions of foot Cossacks of the Black Sea; the regiment of Boutirsk, of our division, arrived from Taman, where it had been under the orders of the Ataman of the Don Cossacks; afterwards the 1st brigade of the 14th division entered the town. The garrison might be estimated at about 35,000 men including sailors.

The troops were distributed as follow:—On the bastions 5 and 6 were the four reserve and four depôt battalions of the 13th division; our regiment was stationed in the ravine between the bastions 4 and 5; the regiment of Moscow of the 1st brigade of our division occupied the bastions 1 and 2; the regiment of Boutirsk was placed in the Malakhoff Bastion; the regiment of Borodino was in the bastion 3. When the 1st brigade of the 14th division entered the town the four depôt battalions of the 13th division joined our regiment. The sailors were all armed like infantry soldiers and stationed in all the batteries to work the guns. The foot Cossacks of the Black Sea were distributed among the bastions, in front of which they formed ambuscades.

These Cossacks are called also Plastoons, from the Russian word plast, which means a flat piece of metal, stone, or other substance. They received this name from the extraordinary accuracy with which they fire from their rifles, so that if the target is a hard substance the ball is sure afterwards to be picked up flattened or a plast.

They are certainly very fine troops, and pass all their lives in active warfare with the Cherkess. They have few words of command, but all their movements are directed by signals. These signals are imitations of the cries of different animals found in the Caucasus: they howl like jackals and wolves, bark like dogs, mew like cats, &c. These signals are of course understood by the men. Their appearance in Sevastopol was anything but prepossessing, as their clothes were in tatters, so that in many places the bare skin was to be seen through the holes of their garments. If they tear their clothes amongst the mountains, they might, for the sake of humanity and decency, have been better dressed while in the Crimea. The most extraordinary force in the town were the convicts, who, in their ordinary dress, minus the chains, were formed into a kind of forlorn hope; they were armed with cold arms only, such as long-handled axes, boarding-pikes, &c.

The time from our entering the town up to the opening of the bombardment, 17th October, we passed monotonously enough,—working at the batteries and mounting guard in the town when our turn came round. One day the surgeon of our regiment, Lebedieff, related to me that he had been to see the wounded of the battle of Alma, lying in the naval hospital. This was soon after we entered the town, the second or third day; when, to his horror, he found the place fall of wounded men who had never had their wounds dressed from the day of the Alma, except such dressings as they could make themselves by tearing up their own shirts. The moment he entered the room he was surrounded by a crowd of these miserable creatures, who had recognised him as a doctor; some of whom held out muti-lated stumps of arms wrapped up in dirty rags, and crying out to him for assistance. The stench of the place was dreadful, and he learned that after they had arrived from the Alma they were all put into this hospital, where they had seen no one except the soldiers who gave them food, or carried out such of their com-rades as death had relieved from their sufferings.

Dr. Lebedieff, for the sake of humanity, attended to as many of them as he could, choosing the worst cases, and performed several amputations with such instruments as he could find in the hospital; but when he turned to go away, fatigued and dis-gusted with the authorities for letting these poor wretches rot in their wounds, such a number to whom he had not been able to attend thrust themselves before him, that with difficulty he could tear himself away, and then only with a promise to return. These unfortunate men were a fortnight without having their wounds dressed!

The works advanced rapidly. The colonel of engineers, Totleben, visited all the bastions every day to see that the officers did their duty, and that the works were carried on correctly. The profile of the batteries was in general small, with the exception of bastions 3 and 4, which were both situated on the summit of steep ascents. When the trenches of the enemy were begun, Totleben was almost constantly on the bastions, observing their progress and direction, at the same time changing his own plan to meet theirs to advantage, so that the form of the batteries was sometimes altered two or three times. As an instance of this, when Totleben remarked a salient angle of the French trenches opposite the southern *lunette* of the bastion No. 5, he immediately threw up a battery behind this lunette, near the barracks, that enfiladed a part of this trench, while the breastwork of a part of the bastion 4 was thrown back, and six guns of large calibre placed there that bore perpendicularly on the same point, so that this angle of the trench was perfectly commanded.

These were the tactics of Totleben. Whenever he remarked the works of the enemy advancing, he immediately made some change to meet them. Sometimes this object was gained by simply changing the position of a gun, or by altering an embrasure to bear upon the point required. If the object could not be attained by either of these means, the whole battery was re-made. This it was that rendered difficult the prosecution of a regular siege against an unfortified place, as it enabled the engineer to erect his defences according to the attacks of the enemy. The taking of a regularly-built fortress may always be calculated with some degree of certainty by knowing the strength and means of the besieging army, as in that case nothing can be changed, but the walls can be battered down and the place taken by assault through the breach, effected. When, as in this case, the defenders erect works against the attacking army, with the immense resources that the town contained, it was impossible for a regular siege to make much progress.

On the 4th of October the regiments forming the garrison of Sevastopol were ordered to send their riflemen outside the works, in order to prevent a too near approach of the franctireurs of the enemy. The men of our regiment occupied the ground in front of bastion 4, and the ravine between that and bastion 5. These riflemen were in small holes, or behind stones, anywhere for shelter.

One of the men of our regiment, Ivan Grigorieff, lying behind a stone, took a shot at a French soldier who was lying before him only partly concealed, and missed him; he acknowledged the compliment by waving his cap, and immediately fired at Grigorieff, who acknowledged it by standing on his head and waving his legs, in token that he was unhurt. It was a very pretty sight from the bastions to see the two lines of *franc-tireurs*, marked by little puffs of white smoke, as they lay and comfortably took shots at each other; something amusing happened almost every day. Our men had orders to fire at anything visible, no matter what the distance.

About this time preparations were made to place two mortars near the six guns bearing upon the French trench above mentioned. The ground was levelled, the platforms made, and the mortars brought up and placed ready to open fire. But when the mortars came to be tried, it was discovered that the touchhole of one of them was completely spoiled, so that it was impossible to use it, while the other was useless, because, being of an old form, and the shells of a new construction, the latter would not enter the mortar. All this labour was lost; the mortars were thrown aside and replaced by others. This is the way they do things in the Russian army.

On the 13th of October the trenches were to be seen at a distance around all the bastions, when Admiral Korniloff, about 11 o'clock in the forenoon, ordered a cannonade to be opened from all the guns for an hour. A red flag was hoisted from bastion 4, where the Admiral himself was, as a signal to the other bastions, which they all repeated, and then a tremendous cannonade was opened on all sides. At this time I was with my company at work at a battery in the second line that was afterwards called the battery of Captain Sherinsky Shakhmatoff, from the name of its commander. It is situated immediately behind bastion 4. I got upon the roof of a house near to admire the sight, which really was very fine, and thence I watched the shot and shell as they pitched. As far as I could remark the shells appeared to fall and burst very well.

After it was over I joined a group of officers about the admiral, who was conversing with them, and pointing out which guns had done well and which badly. Afterwards he said that he intended to send out fire-ships against the enemy's fleet, but they had placed a steamer opposite the entrance to the harbour only the day previous, as if they had known of our intentions. I saw myself this fire-ship prepared, but know no other reason why no use was made of it. The Russians themselves were in continual fear of fire-ships, which they daily expected, and which might have done them considerable damage. During the cannonade above mentioned the enemy ceased their labours, but the moment it was over they began, like gallant fellows as they were, to repair damages and go on with their work. We could see distinctly the earth as it was thrown out of the trench on to the breastwork, and many were astonished at the quantity thrown up at each shovelful, saying that the enemy was digging his trenches by means of machines. We had an opportunity soon afterwards of inspecting the English shovels, as a number of them were taken in the Turkish redoubt at the battle of Balaclava, when we were much astonished at the superiority they possessed over ours; but we soon learnt to conclude that in England there could be no such thing as peculation.

All regimental tools in Russia are kept in store, to be shown when required, but not for use; they are painted annually, and the colonel pockets a considerable sum every year for the repairs and renewing such as he thinks ought to be worn out. When they come to be used they are good for nothing. In my company the men broke all their tools after three days' work, and we in consequence were obliged to get new ones, which were little better.

Admiral Korniloff arranged that a cannonade should be opened for two hours every other day, while Admiral Novosilsky, who commanded bastion 4, advised that it should take place daily, as that would keep the enemy on the qui vive.

On the 14th nothing of any interest occurred, we were all hard at work on the batteries.

The 15th a cannonade was opened from the batteries of the town that lasted from twelve till two, during which a gun burst in bastion 4 and another in bastion 5, killing and wounding several men. About 1 o'clock we were all surprised to hear the sea-batteries open fire, and on looking in that direction we could see a vessel that appeared to be a transport drifting towards the harbour. She was taken for a fire-ship, and all the batteries opened fire upon her, and, as I learned afterwards, fired 2500 rounds, out of which only three struck the vessel, which afterwards bore up and ran under Fort Alexander and No. 10 battery (Quarantine), when a steamer belonging to the allied fleet came out for the purpose of towing her off, but, after exchanging shots with the forts, retired, and the vessel drifted into Peschannoi Bay, and went on shore. The crew of this vessel are said to have escaped in the boat when they saw her drifting towards the formidable batteries. It was absurd to expend so much ammunition without effecting the object of sinking the ship.

CHAPTER 5

The Assault

On the 16th of October our regiment finished the battery behind the bastion 4. This battery was in the second line and called the Sherinsky Shakhmatoff battery. Now the enemy's sharpshooters began to draw nearer to the batteries, that rendered working in them more perilous than before; we could also see the trenches all round us, and the embrasures of an English battery could be distinguished to the left of our bastion, In the evening our battalion relieved the 2nd battalion of our regiment, stationed behind the stone wall, between the bastions 4 and 5. We were under the orders of Captain Zorine of the navy, and belonged to bastion 4 that was commanded by Admiral Novosilsky. All the bastions and batteries around the town were commanded by officers of the navy, with the exception of bastion 5, which was under the command of Major-General Oslonovich, who was soon afterwards succeeded by Major-General Timofeyeff. The garrison was commanded by Lieutenant-General Von Möller, while the commander of our division lived unknown and unnoticed, as doubtless Prince Menschikoff had discovered by this time that he was useless.

It was the duty of our battalion to furnish the advance sentries, for which duties volunteers were called for, but as few presented themselves we were obliged to tell off the required number of men. I and Ensign Plousky volunteered to go with the men, and Captain Gové was appointed to inspect our line.

As soon as it was dark we left the lines, and posted our sentries across the ravine between the bastions 4 and 5, at a distance in advance of about 500 yards, communicating on our left with the sailors from bastion 4 and on our right with the regiment of Minsk from bastion 5.

During the night several shells were thrown from the mortars in the bastions, from which the splinters reached us and killed one of my men. About 10 o'clock the work in the enemy's trenches was carried on with extraordinary vigour; I could hear, from where I stood, every stroke of their tools: shortly after this we could hear rattling as of heavy vehicles passing over the ground. In advance of us there were some Cossacks of the Black Sea in ambuscade. A non-commissioned officer of the Cossacks came to report to me that the enemy had opened a new trench opposite us, and that a large quantity of transport was moving about the trenches. I sent this man to the bastion, that he might be able to point out the places at which these works were carried on.

On the return of the Cossack I left my sentries in charge of Ensign Plousky, and went with him to the Cossack ambuscade; the last 100 yards of our journey was down hill, and, not to be perceived by the enemy, we were obliged to crawl on our bellies. The ambuscade was in a ravine behind a small hillock, as the Cossacks told me, about 250 yards from the French sentries. It appeared to me not to be half that distance, as we could see them moving about and hear their conversation. At a short distance in the rear of the sentries we could see the men working at the trench. We all lay as still as death, afraid to move, as the rattling of a firelock would at once have discovered us. I did not remain here more than a quarter of an hour, as I considered myself far too near the enemy and too far from my duty to feel easy, and I breathed more freely after I had climbed the hill and knew myself to be out of sight of the enemy, as I had no idea of making a useless sacrifice of myself.

About 2 o'clock Captain Gové brought us the order from General Oslonovich to retire into the town, as he intended to open a cannonade from all the guns of the place. This was also communicated to the naval officer in charge of the sentries to the left of our line. This officer flatly refused to obey the order, saying that he was before the bastion 4, which was commanded by Admiral Novosilsky, and that he knew nothing about General Oslonovich, who had no right to order him when to retire. Captain Gové reported to the general that the sailors refused to obey his orders. He raged and stormed, but eventually ordered us to occupy the same position as before, putting off the cannonade till some more convenient opportunity. Whether the naval officer was right in refusing obedience to the General I do not know, but great disorder and confusion reigned throughout the town. Everybody seemed to do what he thought best.

A little before daybreak we could hear the drums and bugles of the enemy. As the day began to break we all retired into the town by the order of the commander of the battalion. I then went with Plousky to a traktir, near the theatre, to get some tea; but here they were all asleep, and before hot water could be procured we heard a tremendous cannonade opened, but, as I knew that orders had been given to fire from the bastions every alternate day, I could easily account for this firing. Besides, I thought it probable that the works that had been carried on the preceding night might have caused the batteries of the town to open. While I was proving in this way to my comrade that it was from the bastions, a round shot pitched into the courtyard of the house, and killed two fowls, which convinced us at once that the bombardment was at last opened. On looking towards the fields the sight was a very pretty one, for little puffs of smoke were continually showing themselves in positions where we least expected to find a battery. By the time we got out of the house on to the Place du Théâtre, a great number of soldiers, sailors, convicts, and others, were running for their lives away from the batteries. We asked them what was the matter and where they were going?

Their only answer was, "The Frenchman has opened fire!" and on they ran in a state of complete panic. We hurried off to join our men, whom we found with all the regiment under arms, in order to keep them from running away. Indeed, the unexpected opening of the bombardment seemed to have struck every one with such a panic, that almost all were ready to run to places of safety. The first killed and wounded were being carried away from the batteries, some on stretchers, others on litters made of firelocks, while many were carried away in sacks. It took some time before the confusion that reigned throughout the town could be brought into order sufficient to answer to the fire of the Allies. All working parties were sent back to their quarters. I was stationed with my company at the end of the Place du Théâtre in the ravine between bastions 4 and 5. The other three companies of our battalion were stationed immediately behind the breastwork, while the rest of the regiment was on the Place du Théâtre. The theatre itself was turned into a field hospital for our regiment. I got with my company as closely under the hill of the bastion 4 as I could, as we suffered more from the fire of the English that came over it than we did from that of the French.

It was very slow work standing here doing nothing, so I went to the 3rd battalion that was about 150 yards behind us in the street leading to the Place du Théâtre. With the officers of this battalion I found the commanding officer of the convicts, who was relating with immense enthusiasm the prowess of his men, and their devotion to the cause, though many of them refused to take any part in the defence of the town, and were sent into the interior. A ship left Kamiesch Bay with her yards and rigging in disorder, and took the direction of Eupatoria; this, the officer of convicts informed us, was a sign that some important personage of the allied fleet or army must be dead. We therefore concluded that this vessel was employed to transport to France the remains of Marshal St. Arnaud, as we had heard that he was dead.

About 2 o'clock we began to observe the bombardment from the sea, though the smoke around the town was so thick that we could see nothing of the ships; the town suffered a good deal from the ships, but few of the shot reached us—we had enough of our own as it was!

The town at this time was a perfect hell, as from all sides were flying shot as thick as hail, and from the ships shells, round and cylindrical. These latter were objects of great respect and interest, and many of them that did not burst were carefully examined by the curious. A description of these shells had been previously given in the Russian papers from some found after the bombardment of Odessa. The frightful din, smoke, groans and cries of the wounded as they were carried from the batteries, and the confusion that reigned, rendered the place the most horrible it is possible to conceive.

About 3 o'clock the powder magazine in a French battery was blown up by a discharge from the *lunette* of bastion 5, and there was a loud hurrah throughout the town at this triumph. Our commanders immediately organised a sortie of volunteers to destroy this battery and spike the guns. From our battalion there were twenty-five men of whom I had the command, some sailors of the 29th sea company (*équipage*), as well as some of the convicts. These were under the orders of Lieutenant Novikoff of the navy. We started, I should think, a little before 4 o'clock on this sortie, and the bastion 4 opened a heavy fire of grape for a short time before we left the defences, which caused the riflemen to keep out of the way.

Our superior officers thought that this expedition would have been very easy and practicable, as they supposed the French battery was deserted after the explosion took place there an hour before, as not another shot was fired from it afterwards. We were divided into three small columns; that on the left flank was under my orders. It was arranged that the two flank columns should attack first, and that the centre should come up to their support.

We went out of the fortifications by the ravine between bastions 4 and 5, and were obliged to make half a turn to the right in order to gain the hill on which was placed the French battery we were to attack. The flank columns had not time to reach their object before Lieutenant Novikoff appeared before the trench with the centre. He was allowed to approach to within a short distance of the trench, when a heavy fire of rifles was opened upon his column. By this manoeuvre the flank columns were discovered. My party became exposed to a cross fire, and, being on the left, I was the farthest from the fortifications, and ran the greatest danger of being cut off. Besides, I was also the farthest of all from the French battery, and had been met long before any resistance was expected. So I decided to retire, and the men agreed with me unanimously, for they immediately turned back.

The centre column alone reached the battery, and found in front of it a trench filled with riflemen, who soon caused them to retire without affecting anything. I lost nine men out of my party; two were left dead on the spot, but the others contrived to follow us though wounded. On my return the commander of the battalion asked what we had done.

"Nothing!" said I.

"How nothing?" repeated he.

"In this way: we were not more than sixty men in the open ground, while there were at least 200 French in the trench before the battery which everyone thought was deserted."

"Have you brought all your men back?" asked he.

"No; two are left behind, as we had no means of carrying them; they were both killed." In retreating we were obliged to run from stone to stone and crouch, but the moment we showed ourselves we were sure to be shot at.

It was extraordinary how small an amount of damage was done to the sea-batteries by the allied fleet; but I suppose this was because the ships were stationed at too great a distance from them to do them any harm.

The number of killed and wounded in battery No. 10 was only twenty-seven, and one gun disabled, and this after a furious cannonade of about five hours. This battery too was one of the most exposed. Fort Constantine, I heard, suffered more than any of the others, and if the cannonade had lasted another hour it was the general opinion that it would have been battered down.

Besides, I believe the garrison had almost exhausted their powder, so that only a few rounds more were left. I heard that to this fort was opposed the ship of the English Admiral Lyons. About 5 o'clock a large magazine of flour belonging to the Government was set on fire by a shell from the fleet; and all the men that could be spared were sent to extinguish it, at the head of whom was Lieutenant Novikoff, then just returned from the sortie, but they only succeeded in saving a portion of the damaged flour.

About six o'clock the rumour began to spread that Admiral Korniloff had been wounded on his favourite spot—the Malakhoff hill; his right leg had been carried off, and there were little hopes of saving his life. This was all passed from one to another in whispers, as it was forbidden to speak openly of this event, as Korniloff was much respected and beloved by all belonging to the town, of which he was regarded as the chief defence, and his death would have a very discouraging effect, especially upon the sailors. He had done much already towards the preservation of the town by the coolness with which he carried all his plans into operation. Many felt deep sorrow when they heard of the death of this favourite Admiral; We were all heartily glad when as the evening drew on the enemy ceased firing, for we had been pounded from six in the morning till seven in the evening, and began to get very tired of the amusement.

It was fortunate for us that the Allies sent no shells on the first day, only round shot, which do not occasion half the damage the shells do, for when they once lodge in a wall or elsewhere there is an end of them. Lucky were we, too, that during the night we were undisturbed, as that allowed us time to get a little rest and to repair the damages done to the fortifications. After the firing had ceased I found that I had lost out of my company twenty men killed and wounded. What the losses were in the different batteries I am unable to say; but they must have been very great, as the whole of the garrison was without any cover and consequently exposed to all the fire in large masses.

The barracks that were in bastion 4, and especially those in front, were completely ruined. Much of the breastwork too had suffered, while the embrasures looked like great holes; but this was not extraordinary when it is remembered that they were not revetted, but the cheeks were simply plastered with clay. On the bastion 3 the men at the guns had been changed three times during the day, not for the purpose of giving the first a little Test, but because they were no longer in existence. The powder magazine was blown up—that destroyed forty men; the bastion itself was completely destroyed. The upper story of the Malakhoff tower was ruined. It was a general subject of remark in the town that the English fired much better than the French on this day,

There was little rest for any of us that night. Half my company was obliged to work at the batteries repairing the damages done during the day, while I set the other half to work to make us some shelter for the next day, which we effected by throwing up a slight epaulement, behind which we could crouch, while over our heads we stretched an old sail to keep the sun from us. The shelter this afforded was not very great, but still we were not quite so exposed, and the next day's cannonade we supported much better.

During the day scarcely anybody could be seen about the streets, but now the whole town was alive. Some ran to satisfy the cravings of their appetites, others to pay visits of *adieu* to their friends, while others again made their way to the different field hospitals to see, perhaps for the last time, some friend who had been wounded during the day, perhaps lost a leg or an arm. In either of these cases little hopes could be entertained of their recovery, as we had few surgeons of experience in the town; the greater number were young students from the different universities, who had not finished their term of studies by about a year and a half. So great had been the demand for surgeons for the army from the beginning of the war, that they were glad to get anyone; besides Nicholas had said he would have them, and there they were.

In our regiment we had one of these youngsters, who had no idea how he was to set about an operation of any kind, and now he had some of the most serious kind entrusted to him. Under these circumstances it was not at all extraordinary if few of the wounded ever recovered. There were some, however, who did recover, but they were for the most part those who merely pretended to be wounded that they might be out of harm's way.

After the battle of the Alma we had some instances of this practice, and Captain Volkhoff, who then reported himself, did the same now, saying, "Why should I remain to be killed, when I have a wife and children?" But it must not be forgotten, as I said before, that he was the son of the colonel, who, when there were any rewards to be distributed, found no one among the officers so deserving as his son.

During the whole day I had fasted, so about eleven o'clock at night I went to Schneider's hotel to get something to stop the cravings of hunger. Here I found a large party of officers who were drinking and relating the different gallant deeds each had performed on that day. When I left the hotel, many were evidently under the influence of wine and preparing terrible things for the Allies the next day. On my return I still found my company at work, for there was no rest for anyone in the town that night. There were still a good many of the inhabitants in the town who had not been able to get away before, or, as in some instances, preferred remaining. There were, too, a great many ladies still in the town: among them was the wife of Lieutenant-Colonel Khloponine, No. 5 Light Battery, of 17th Artillery Brigade, who would not leave her husband; she was with him at the bivouac on the Alma and in the town during all the time his battery remained there. All these people, mixed with soldiers, sailors, officers, &c, formed motley groups about the streets in the darkness, where they discussed the events of the day past with anxious and gloomy anticipations of the one to follow.

By daylight on the morning of the 18th of October we were all in our places in expectation of the fatal hour. At six o'clock the cannonade again commenced. This day was an important one in our regiment, as it was that of St. Thomas, our patron saint. Why he was our patron I never could understand, but an image of him was always carried with the regiment. About nine o'clock the whole of the regiment, except the battalion to which I belonged, was paraded on the Place du Théâtre for the purpose of celebrating Holy Mass in the presence of the general of division. The priest performed his sacred duty without giving the slightest heed to the shot that were continually whistling over and about him, though many of the others were paying more attention to the direction in which the shot might pitch than to the words of the priest, who at the Alma administered the Communion to many, a poor fellow while exposed to a hot fire.

After the Mass, the general of division went to the colonel's quarters to drink success to the regiment and its future victories in sparkling champagne, while the colonel sent out ten bottles of wine to the officers of each battalion. It must not be supposed, however, that this was an act of spontaneous generosity, for the colonel is always allowed a sum of money to keep up the regimental holiday. There was a great deal of wrangling among the officers about this wine, as many of the seniors wished to take more than their share; for there is nothing of that feeling of union that I have since found to exist in the English army, among the officers of a Russian regiment.

About eleven o'clock we heard a great noise on the Place du Théâtre. Our battalion was still where it was the day before, i.e. behind the wall connecting the bastions 4 and 5. On my inquiry what was the matter—"An alarm! The enemy is coming!" shouted a soldier, running towards the commander of the battalion. I ordered my men under arms, and to advance towards the wall; for my company formed a kind of reserve to the other three, and had the defence of the gateway that had been left in the wall entrusted to it in case of an assault. No sooner had I told the men to advance than they all broke into a run towards the wall, leaving me behind. It must not be thought that over-anxiety to meet their enemies caused these men to run;—no, they were only anxious to reach the little shelter that was afforded by the small breastwork in front of the gateway. I must confess I felt very much annoyed at this conduct of my men, but

I could not stop them.

We remained in expectation of the enemy about a quarter of an hour, but as he did not come, we went back to our places. It was a mistake, we were told. We thought the alarm had been a signal from the observatory that the Allies were advancing, as from that point a lookout was kept that watched all that took place in the trenches.

About an hour after this we had another alarm, but a *bonâ fide* one this time. The telegraph sent information that columns of the enemy were visible. My company was again ordered to advance to the wall, but not wishing them to run again, I brought them up at a slow march, much to their annoyance, as the rifle-balls just reached us. This time, however, I brought my men up in perfect order, and placed them as much under cover as I could, when we were again ordered to retire to our place. This proves we were constantly in expectation of the assault during the first days of the bombardment, nor were we over-confident in ourselves, so that it would not have been difficult to have got into the town then, and once in, the defence would have been over.

We were frequently alarmed by the loud hurrahs that took place in different parts of the town, and that followed any well-directed shot or an explosion.

On this day Admiral Korniloff was buried near the library within the foundation of a new church, where had previously been buried Admiral Lazareff, who had commanded before Korniloff the Black Sea fleet, This foundation is about level with the surface, a little above the library on the other side of the street.

I am sorry that I am not able to relate what passed in other parts of the town, but the position in which I was placed entirely excluded me from seeing what was going on in the Karabelnaya or other portions of the town, save the one in which I was.

During the night we were again left undisturbed by the Allies, so were enabled to effect, with perfect ease, the repairs of the batteries, and prepare better cover for ourselves, for the rifle-balls had begun to make us very uncomfortable,

On the third day of the cannonade the fire was particularly hot, as the Allies began to throw in shell, which we had not hitherto seen. I suppose that during the first two days the mortars were not ready. In a confined space a shell is perhaps the most destructive thing that can be employed, and frequently one would put from ten to twenty-five men *hors de combat*. Some were daring enough to rush upon them as they fell, draw the fuse, and thus prevent their bursting, thereby saving the lives of their comrades; whoever did this immediately received the cross of St. George, which is only given for rare examples of courage, and is of the utmost importance to the men, as it exempts them from corporal punishment, and gives them an increase of pay.

On this day Captain Zorine, of the navy, ordered a man to be punished for theft, which was done by tying the man to a cooled gun, and while the bombardment was going on, he received about 150 lashes with rope's ends in the presence of his comrades and Captain Zorine, his commander, who paid not the slightest attention to the shot and shell that were flying about very plentifully in all directions, for this interesting ceremony took place about 2 o'clock in the day. I witnessed it myself.

Our days began to be very monotonous, as we were obliged to remain in one place from daybreak till the evening, and the nights were spent in repairing the batteries, constructing new ones, or in improving the cover for the men. From the 19th the Allies began to fire at night, when we did not care so much for the shells, as we could easily trace their course by the burning of the fuse. Besides, the firing was not at all rapid, and our men on the lookout had become accustomed to the duty, so that we heard continually that the shells were going to the right, left, or beyond us; but when they were upon us it was .all helter-skelter to find some place of safety, for we had no case-mates in those days, nor was it easy to escape the vertical fire, particularly the round shot, as those we could not see or hear till they were too near to avoid them; they did a great deal of damage during the night, as then the people ventured more out of their cover.

No lights were allowed in the town, or on the batteries, as that always afforded an aim for the Allies, of which they were not slow to avail themselves. The very soldiers were afraid to light their pipes, not to draw down upon themselves the fire of the enemy. All the works at the batteries were carried on with as little noise as possible. The people moved about the town as if afraid their footsteps would betray their presence to the enemy. Little was to be heard, save the warning voice of the lookout. We suffered much from the rifle-balls that, fired at a great elevation, fell almost perpendicularly on to the heads of the men crowded behind the defences.

General Totleben, with a mounted orderly, rode daily through all the batteries of the town, giving orders and directions what was to be done during the ensuing night. His coolness and self-control on these occasions are above all praise. At each bastion there was an officer, whose duty it was to watch the works of the enemy, and report daily their direction and progress to Totleben; besides these, a. tower had been built near the ladies' school, not very far from the library, where a constant lookout was kept, and where the generals charged with the defence of the town took their stations. From the information thus obtained Totleben carried on the defence which has gained him immortal honour.

This war has proved that the best kind of defence against a regular attack consists of earthworks, that can so easily be changed, altered, and increased to meet the attacks. The batteries at Sevastopol were at first nothing but earth, loosely thrown up with the shovel, the embrasures were plastered with moistened clay, but when it was discovered that this was not enough, they were faced with stout wicker work. Then fascines were introduced, and finally gabions were employed. The batteries were frequently found not to bear upon the required point, or the embrasures were not made so as to enable the guns to be pointed in the right direction.

Whenever a discovery of this sort was made the whole was changed during the night. If no changes were required, new and more formidable works were added. In this respect Sevastopol offered unexampled advantages in the arsenal, so that there were always guns to mount in these new works. If one of the bastions of Sevastopol were to be taken, and a section made, suppose for instance of the Malakhoff, it could then be traced through its different phases of existence, till it became the mass of sand-bags and gabions it is at present, with the enormous embrasures firmly revetted with two and three rows of gabions. Then were added the case-mates—holes dug in the ground, and covered with enormous ship-timber that was again covered with earth to the thickness of eight or ten feet, and perfectly proof to the heaviest bomb. In these the garrison, and a part of the gunners could always find shelter; though these case-mates eventually caused the loss of the Malakhoff, and consequently of the whole town. By this means of defence it was possible to concentrate a tremendous fire upon any given point of the trenches, The commander of every bastion and every battery had his orders in what direction he was to fire, and what guns. All these arrangements emanated from Totleben,

With a stone fortress the case is very different, for to that nothing can be added, nor can anything be altered. Once possess a plan of the place, and conduct the attack upon a regular system, always supposing your army to be strong enough, and it is not difficult to calculate the time required to reduce the place; for any damage you may cause is permanent, and not, as in the case of earthworks, to be repaired or even improved during the night.

But it must not be supposed that I think regular fortresses are useless; on the contrary I think that every well-regulated country, especially if it have unpleasant neighbours, ought to possess regular fortresses on all the strategical points, I am afraid I have rather wandered from my subject.

During the time I was in the town, I made with my company three batteries, and four powder magazines. The first battery was in the second line behind bastion 4; the second was in front of the salient angle of bastion 4, and mounted four guns; and the third was among the houses behind the theatre, and mounted five guns. While at work on these batteries I frequently had the honour of receiving directions from Totleben himself about the manner in which the embrasures were to be made, and the direction they were to take; the sailors made the platforms for these batteries.

On the 20th our battalion was relieved by the 4th battalion of our regiment, while we took our station on the Place du Théâtre with the rest of the regiment. We found the life here far more pleasant than in the front line, for, without counting that we were safe from rifle-balls, we had pretty comfortable quarters in the houses about the theatre, and especially the house of the Post-office—the postmaster having quitted the town in such a hurry or fright that he had left the whole of the furniture and utensils in the house, with a piano among other articles. Sometimes we used to collect around this instrument, and while one played, the others danced or sang, making so much noise that the whistling of the shot and shell could be no longer heard.

The commanders of the battalions were in the next house in the lower story for the sake of greater safety. A part of the men were in the houses too, but by far the greater part were in the street, nor were they allowed to enter the houses from the fear that they might stray, as we were hourly in expectation of the assault. We remained here till the 26th; the days were monotonous enough, but it was something to be under a roof again, while the soldiers who were in the streets crowded and crouched under the wall, thinking that was the safest place, but if a shell had been dropped occasionally amongst them-the casualties would not have been few.

On the 21st a bridge of vessels was thrown across the southern harbour; but the vessels were found to suffer much from the enemy's fire, so they were afterwards changed for rafts which shells or shot could not hurt.

All the firelocks were piled in front of the trottoir, while we were stationed near the theatre; when, one day, I think the 22nd, several round shot rolled in one after the other and destroyed about thirty firelocks in my company alone. After this we got orders to lay them down, when we lost less. We lost very few men at this time; upon an average not more than three men per company a-day, and some days a company never lost a man; officers were seldom killed, as they were better able to take care of themselves. During the night we used to go on fatigue duly to work at the batteries.

On the night of the 21st-22nd, General Oslonovich sent a sortie out of bastion 5 to the cemetery without informing the commanders of the other bastions what he had done. The column was seen and fired into by the enemy, General Oslonovich, hearing the firing, and forgetting all about the sortie he had sent out, inquired of a sentry what was the matter. The sentry, of course, knew nothing, so General Oslonovich ordered a cannonade to be opened in the direction of the firing, which was soon taken up by bastion 6 that blazed away furiously at the sortie. A soldier soon afterwards came running to say that they were firing at their own people. This was told to General Oslonovich, who ordered the firing to cease, and sent to bastion 6 to inform them that their own men were before them, which he had previously forgotten to do. Twenty-four men and three officers fell victims to this blunder, and the whole column of volunteers returned, leaving eight dead bodies behind them. These bodies remained in full view of the batteries all the next day as an encouragement to others to volunteer for sorties and be killed from the guns that ought to protect them. The Russians were too proud to send a flag of truce to bury these men, so the next night their bodies were brought into the town. All who were killed in the defence of the town were buried on the north side of the harbour.

On the 22nd the number of sick began sensibly to increase; the diseases were chiefly of the class of diarrhoea brought on from the following causes:—up to the 19th the soup for the soldiers' dinners and suppers was generally made on the spot, in the streets, under the walls of the houses. On this day, as a whole company was waiting around the kettle for supper, which was almost ready, a round shot plumped into the middle of the mess, and, knocking a great hole in the bottom of the kettle, let all the contents through upon the fire, so that the poor fellows were obliged to go supperless to their work. At this time the men used to eat their so called, dinner at daybreak, when they left their work.

To have it ready by that time it was necessary to begin the cooking soon after midnight, which became impossible when the Allies began after the 19th to keep up the fire at night. In consequence of this, all the food was prepared in Fort Nicholas, and transported in large tubs to the batteries and places where the men were stationed, so that it reached the men quite cold, with fat swimming in large cakes on the top of the soup. Besides this cause, which was a very powerful one, fear I believe to have caused a great deal of sickness, for many of the men calculated that they would soon be killed, so it was useless to eat, and lived almost entirely upon their brandy, of which double portions were now distributed morning and evening.

On the evening of the 25th, just as I had ordered my men to attention, and the sergeant was calling the muster-roll, for we were going on fatigue duty to work at the batteries, a shell pitched on the right flank of the company. The men began to run; I ordered them to lie down, which I felt ashamed to do before my company, so stood within a few yards of our unwelcome visitor in a state of mortal fear, and wondering whether that was ordained to decide my fate, when to my great surprise and joy the fuse went out and the danger was past. I ordered the men up again, and we began to move to the right, when another shell came through the air with its peculiar shou-shouing, and pitched about three yards in front of the company. Some of the men threw themselves on the ground, while I remained standing, not knowing in fact what to do, for I thought that, having escaped one, the second would be sure to burst and single me out for its victim. Besides I thought that we must have been remarked from the enemy's batteries and they were sending these gentle reminders that they were aware of our presence. This shell like the former one did not burst! The men got up again and we went on to the battery; while on the road I could hear the soldiers talking over the two events that had just happened. They came to the conclusion that I was a wizard or enchanter, and that if I said to a shell "Burst not!" it would not burst, for they were firmly convinced that I had the power of witchcraft. This is the way a Russian soldier always explains what he cannot understand.

On the 23rd General Liprandi, commander of the 12th division, that had arrived from Bessarabia only the day before, received orders to attack the position of Balaclava on the next day (24th).[1] Liprandi asked permission to put off the attack for one day, that he might have time to reconnoitre the position, and ascertain how the Turkish troops were disposed. This was done; and on the evening of the 24th Liprandi gave his orders in person to everyone from the commanders of battalions up to his generals of brigade, pointing out to each man the position on the plan he was to occupy and at what hour and minute he was to be there.

The plan was to take the redoubt on the hill near the stone bridge that has since received the name of the Traktir bridge from the Allies, and, having gained possession of this redoubt, to enfilade the next redoubt, which would thus be exposed to a cross fire from that and the field batteries. As General Liprandi knew his men were for the most part young soldiers, who had never been in action before, to give them greater firmness and self-reliance, he informed the regiment of Odessa, that was ordered to attack the first redoubt, that he would send behind them two field-pieces loaded with canister, with orders to open fire upon them if they should waver or attempt to turn back. He kept his word, for the guns were there, though they were not required, because the regiment took the redoubt. General Liprandi gained his object; if he employed severe measures, no doubt he considered them necessary, for he is perhaps one of the

---

1. The village of Chorgoun had been occupied by the regiment of Vladimir up to the arrival of the 12th division. The 12th division advanced into the Crimea by forced marches, leaving their knapsacks and other baggage at Perekop.

best generals Russia possesses. He is celebrated for his energy and coolness as well as for being a good tactician.[2]

What rendered the attack of General Liprandi more easy was that the cavalry picket of the Allies that had been established at Kamara was withdrawn on the night of the 24th-25th. The prizes of this action were sixty English cavalry, a large quantity of entrenching and sapping tools, and about sixteen iron guns of a small calibre, as was published in Orders. This was not known in the town till the 27th, and the news was greeted by tremendous cheering from all the batteries that lasted nearly a quarter of an hour.

On the 26th, at 4 p.m., a strong sortie was arranged from the Malakhoff and bastion 3, consisting of the regiments of Boutirsk and Borodino. What was the object of this sortie I could never learn, though it was said at the time that the enemy was attacked in the rear at Balaclava, and that these troops were sent out to try him in front. Whatever the object may have been it evidently failed, as the officer in command of the sortie, Colonel Fedoroff, colonel of the regiment of Boutirsk, was wounded at the first shots, and as no one else knew the object of the sortie they were obliged to retire.

It now became necessary to adopt some means of communication between the town and the batteries, as the rifle-balls reached far beyond the outworks, and caused much damage among the men engaged in transporting ammunition, &c. So it was resolved to connect all the batteries by means of a trench, which, as the Allies did not assault the place, was at length completed and afforded good protection to the men, which became necessary, as it was evident the Allies had resolved upon conducting a regular siege.

On the 26th and 27th our battalion occupied the old place near the wall between the bastions 4 and 5, This was now not

2. The Cossack battery and No. 7 battery of 12th Artillery brigade especially distinguished themselves in this affair by the extreme rapidity with which they fired, as they did not wait to sponge their guns after each round, but after each four or six rounds. The infantry did its duty; but the cavalry covered itself with shame that ten years will never wipe out.

the most agreeable place in the world, for the rifle-balls came in very thick and caused several casualties in my company. Once during this time one of our men was repairing his boot, while before him another soldier lay asleep, when a shell pitched and rolled under the sleeping man. The other, who was at work, remarked that it was a round shot, so that when he awoke his comrade would see what a present he had received during his nap. He had scarcely time to say this before the shell burst and blew the sleeper to atoms: his grey great-coat was found about two hundred yards from the spot, and it was not till the evening that they collected the different parts of his body, for his legs had flown one way and his arms another. The soldier who was at work was untouched.

On the 28th, 29th, and 30th, our battalion was again stationed on the Place du Théâtre. Our regimental surgeon was once taking tea with the Catholic priest, who lived in the same building that is called the Catholic Church, when a round shot burst through the ceiling of the room they were sitting in and fell on the head of the surgeon, killing him on the spot, while the priest escaped unhurt.

On the 29th and 30th I was ordered with my company to make a new roof to the powder-magazine, that was situated on the slope of the hill from bastion 4 towards bastion 5. To do this my men were obliged to bring up ship-timber from the barracks; but the most ticklish part of the operation was the taking off the old roof, which consisted only of thin planks slightly covered with earth. We had hardly got the old roof down before the Allies began to send us shells more often and with greater accuracy than before, so that almost every shell pitched just before or just beyond the magazine, which we were able to cover with three feet of earth without any serious accident, except the loss of a few men. Had a single shell fallen into the magazine itself, we must have all been destroyed, for besides shells there were upwards of sixty poods of powder in it (the *pood* is 36 lbs.).

About two o'clock on the 28th, as there were about six officers in the room of the commander of the battalion, who were some sitting and some lying down after dinner, a shell broke through the roof and two ceilings into the room where they were collected, and burst before reaching the floor. Lieutenant Krasnik, who was sitting near the window, was killed by a splinter, and the others were nearly smothered in lime and plaster, while the room was filled with smoke and gas. The major, with the other officers, came to us in the post-house for shelter; they all washed, and the major went into a back room.

In the front room, before the open window, were seated two cadets of our regiment, looking over the engravings of the Illustrated London News. The Cadet Bouchinsky was sitting in front of the window, and the Cadet Baron Fitengoff was a little on one side. A shell burst in the street, and a splinter flew into the room. Striking the side of the window, it rebounded and carried away the left cheek of Baron Fitengoff, who presented a shocking spectacle, and died three hours afterwards. He was not more than eighteen. The splinter then flew into the opposite corner of the room, where it struck a non-commissioned officer, who was sitting at a table writing, in the chest, and killed him on the spot. The major, hearing the explosion, crept under the table, standing near the wall, to which he crouched as near as possible. At this time I was standing in the doorway between the two rooms. The next day Major Iliashenko reported himself sick, and left the town for the north side.

During a war no officer can resign or get leave of absence on any consideration whatever in the Russian army, so that many who merely entered the service for the sake of something to do, or for fine clothes to wear, were obliged, against their wills, to remain and defend their country.

It must not be supposed, however, that there are no good officers in the Russian army; that idea would be altogether false. The Russians themselves, however, must acknowledge that a considerable proportion of their best officers are men of foreign extraction, such as Poles, Germans, &c. This the men cannot help remarking, and they have in general more confidence in officers who have a good scientific knowledge of their duty. A great many of the officers, too, enter as cadets, knowing nothing whatever of the service, in which they take no interest, They spend their time in drinking, gaming, and other vices, so that, when they are promoted to the rank of officer, after having served the requisite period in the ranks as cadets, they know nothing of their duty, and depend entirely on their non-commissioned officers.

I have seen men of this class nominally in command of companies, while they could do nothing without the sergeant-major, who oppressed and robbed the men with impunity. This state of things causes much suffering, injustice, and discontent among the soldiers, who, however, have no redress. They cannot complain to their captain, as he is under the thumb of the non-commissioned officer, who would not forget the men who had complained of him; they dare not complain to the other authorities, as they would always uphold the cause of officers against the men. It is also a great thing for an officer to study the character of the men under him, and to let them feel that he takes an interest in them, at the same time that he knows his duty, and will allow no one to oppress them. When you have once gained the rude affection and confidence of Russian soldiers, they will follow anywhere; but to do this you must first know their character, and, knowing that, a few words, two or three will do, that will excite some of their few feelings, and they will be cut to pieces for you.

Unfortunately for Russia, few of her officers understand or care to practise this. Russia, too, unlike other nations, can never hope to form officers in the practical school of war, for, as the men who have studied the military art at the different schools are killed or wounded, their places are supplied from the ranks, or from the cadets of the regiment, men whom I have attempted to describe as those who know nothing of their duty, and do not possess sufficient interest in it to learn; besides, all their reasoning faculties are kept down by the severe system of subordination. Whatever a colonel or general says to a subaltern must be law. In all armies, while under arms, implicit obedience must of course be paid to superior officers. I am speaking of when they meet off duty as man to man. Frequently, if a subaltern ventures to give an opinion contrary to his superior, he is reprimanded, and, in some cases, tried for insubordination, with the prospect of a journey to Siberia before him.

While we were in the town we lost twelve officers out of fifty, not by the shot or shell of the Allies, for I do not include those in the twelve, but by sickness. These were all sent to Simpheropol. If the proportion was equal in all the regiments, and I see no reason why it should not be so, the loss in officers must have been very considerable. If to these are added those who were actually killed or wounded, the number would be very large indeed. I am really ashamed to write such things of the men with whom I previously served, but, if I have undertaken to make the British public acquainted with what took place in the Russian army at the beginning of the Crimean campaign, I cannot, in justice to myself, omit so important a fact.

On the 29th a shell fell into the theatre, and burst on the stage, setting fire to the scenery and other inflammable articles. I, with several other officers, was sitting in the box-office of the theatre; we all rushed in to see what was the matter, and saw a very pretty sight—the whole of the scenery on fire; but Colonel Goreff ordered the men to put it out. In the box-office with us was the cadet Kostalsky, who, in his fright at the explosion, broke the window-frame and jumped out.

One of the soldiers of my company, while crossing the Place du Théâtre with a tin full of water, saw a shell fall within a few feet of him; he threw himself upon it, drew out the fuse, and poured the water into the hole. This was the most cool action I think I ever saw, for the man showed great presence of mind. For this action he received the cross of St. George.

On the 30th of October I was sent with my company and two field-pieces to defend the entrance to the town by way of the Woronzow-road at the end of the southern harbour. Rather a poor defence—one company and two guns—if the Allies had thought of entering the town, for the ship that had been previously stationed here was withdrawn.

During the time I was in the town the following occurrence took place. A large quantity of powder was brought up to bastion 4 already made up into charges for the guns. It was all stored carefully in the magazine, and afterwards served put to the guns. A gun was loaded with this powder, shotted ready for firing, when it would not go off. A fresh tube was used with no better result, so the gun was left to be unloaded in the evening. When the powder came to be examined it was dyed millet-seed! Things of this kind have frequently happened. Soldiers have found their cartridges made up with sand instead of powder. This was a part of the peculation carried on. The cartridges and charges are frequently made up for years before they are required for use. It is therefore very difficult to arrive at the real culprits, as they may be dead,, or have left the service, so they escape with impunity. In this instance the effect the discovery had on the men was very great, as they began to exclaim that Menschikoff was a traitor, that this was done expressly that they might all be killed, that he had sold the town, &c. Certain it is that the morale of the men fell considerably after this circumstance.

Something very similar happened in March, 1855, when the attack was made upon Eupatoria. A short time before a number of Greeks had volunteered into the service of Russia, and they were supplied with firelocks and ammunition which, when they came to use at Eupatoria, would not go off. On investigation it was discovered that the cartridges were made up with sand instead of powder. The Greeks thought this was a practical joke played upon them, and they nearly mutinied in consequence. Prince Menschikoff had again to bear all the blame for this as for the millet-seed.

On the evening of the 31st we learnt that the 4th corps had arrived to relieve us, and that this would be our last night in the town. All night we were anxiously expecting the 10th division, but the day broke and they had not arrived.

CHAPTER 6

Inkerman

On the 1st of November we received the order that the 10th division would relieve us at ten o'clock that morning. It would be impossible to describe the joy with which this intelligence was received by both officers and men; we all congratulated ourselves that we had got safely through the fortnight's bombardment, and were again about to enjoy a little fresh country air out of the town. About half-past ten a.m. the regiment of Ekatherinenburg of the 10th division made its appearance to occupy the place of our regiment; it was stationed in the houses of the Bolshaya Morskaya Street. Our regiment moved down towards the Grafsky Prestan and remained on the place behind Fort Nicholas till one o'clock.

Here the men dined, and received four days' provisions. Out of curiosity I went into Fort Nicholas, which I found full of women and children; these were the families of those who did not possess the means of leaving the town, and were all collected here as in a place of safety. Four guns had been placed in the corridor of the fort, in the upper story, and they bore upon the town. On the place behind the fort there were two field batteries, that in case of an assault were to have taken up positions already arranged in the streets. I afterwards went into the assembly-rooms that served as the principal field hospital for the western part of the town. The filth in this place was disgusting.

While I was here, a soldier of the regiment of Ekatherinenburg came up to me, and pointing to a surgeon said, "Is it possible they do such things in your regiment?"

I asked him what was the matter.

"Why," said he, "you see, we had brought in a poor wounded comrade; he was wounded in the knee by a splinter from a shell: the doctor, having examined the wound, began to cut the leg of the wounded man, who cried out, when the doctor struck him in the face for making a noise: it must have hurt him, having his leg cut. I only wish I had my firelock here, I'd pay the doctor out! But he may fall into my hands yet."

I tried to pacify the man by telling him that such things never happened in our regiment. How unfitted must be a man for an army surgeon who has not patience to hear his patients cry out; besides, he was armed with a weapon similar to those I had always seen used for cutting up firewood, but never before for surgical operations. I hurried from the spot disgusted, and thanking Heaven that I had hitherto been spared from falling into the clutches of such a monster. Chloroform was sometimes given to the officers while undergoing an operation, but never to the men.

About one o'clock we embarked from the admiralty in steamers that carried us across to the north side of the harbour. We now learnt that our brigade was to be attached to the column of General Liprandi on the river Chernaya. During the time we were crossing the river, and from the north side, we enjoyed an excellent view of the town and the works of the Allies, and could see distinctly where the shot and shell pitched on both sides. We halted for some time near the barracks, where the colonel, whom we had not seen while in the town, joined the regiment, together with some of the other officers who had skulked from the shot and shell in the town.

At three o'clock we moved across the heights of Mackenzie to the village of Chorgoun, which we reached at eleven o'clock that night, and bivouacked in the open air. The men too were obliged to go without their suppers, as the transport with the camp-kettles, &c, did not arrive till one o'clock. During this march a great many men fell out from fatigue caused chiefly by weakness, brought on by improper nourishment and irregularity while in the town. Many of the men ate little, but drank all they could obtain; they constantly exclaimed that they hoped they would never be wounded; to be killed they did not much object to, but to be wounded, then tormented in the hospital, and to die after all, was a much harder case than to be killed outright. This serves to show the amount of confidence the men had in the hospitals and surgeons.

We slept that night the more soundly that we did not hear the warning voice of the look-out as he shouted "To the right!" "Left!" or "Mind yourselves!" At eleven o'clock on the 2nd of November we crossed the river Chernaya, and took up our position behind the Azoff (Canrobert's) Hill, without crossing the Woronzow road; we consequently formed the left flank of the army of General Liprandi before Balaclava. It began to be rumoured among the officers that we were soon to attack the enemy's position, and that Balaclava was the point chosen for the attack; that is, we were to occupy the hills to the east of Balaclava, and so render the port useless to the English. It was also said that we only awaited the arrival of the Grand Dukes Nicholas and Michael to put this plan into execution.

On this day a colonel arrived to command our regiment, Colonel Gordeieff, from the fifth corps, said to be the nephew of General Luders. Our old colonel, Major-General Volkhoff, was appointed to command a reserve brigade of the Sixth Corps at Moscow.

At four o'clock on the morning of the 3rd we occupied the hills on the left bank of the river, near the stone bridge (Traktir) where the last Turkish redoubt had been; we here succeeded the regiment of Odessa. From the moment we joined the column of General Liprandi we remarked that he was an active, energetic man, and a good General to command troops. We now again began to hear the sound of the drum and music, which since the battle of the Alma we had not heard, as our commanders were afraid to order the morning and evening calls, &c, for fear that they might disturb the slumbers of the enemy. Liprandi also saw that the troops were well fed, for he frequently examined the camp-kettles himself, which prevented the colonels and others from pocketing the men's beef and other provisions,

At half-past five that evening I was sent with my company to occupy the advanced posts. My poor company had always the hardest work to do, of which I alone was the cause, as the major commanding the battalion disliked me as a man of liberal views who thought for himself, though he could find no fault with me for not performing my duty. At seven o'clock that evening an order was received for us to move to the heights above the river Belbek, on the left bank near the stone bridge.

We began our march in a very ill humour, as it began to appear to us that the prince did not know what to do with our regiment, so kept us continually on the move. I started the idea that no doubt the prince expected an attack on that side, and he wished to avail himself of the men who had so distinguished themselves at the Alma by their orderly retreat. I was not wrong in the idea that the prince had not forgiven our general of division for the part he had taken in the battle of the Alma, when by his indecision we all retreated without taking any part in the action.

We arrived on the Belbek about half-past two on the morning of the 4th, and immediately afterwards received the order from Prince Menschikoff's staff to prepare 400 gabions and 200 fascines, which were to be carried to the post-house at Inkerman. As our regiment had never before made either gabions or fascines, officers were chosen who had been educated in corps of cadets, or had previously served in the sappers, in order to instruct the men; I was one of those chosen for this duty; we did not finish our work till eight o'clock in the evening.

Now a rumour, amounting almost to a certainty, became current that we were to attack the Allies, but when, and on which side, no one knew. Preparations for a battle were however visible soon afterwards, for the pouches of the men were examined to see if the number of cartridges was complete, and it was ascertained whether the stretchers were in order, &c. During the evening there had been a rumour that the Grand Dukes Nicholas and Michael had arrived about four o'clock that afternoon; my sergeant assured me that he had seen them himself. About three o'clock on the morning of the 5th the men were ordered to stand to their arms, each man having previously received a single glass of vodka.

We then began to move in the direction of Sevastopol, but nobody knew whither we were going. We only knew that we were advancing to attack the position of the allied army. In this state of ignorance we reached the post-house and there turned to the left; then we could perceive that we must cross the Inkerman Bridge. When we had reached the slope of the hills General Dannenberg, commanding the 4th Army Corps, rode up to us, and, after saluting the men, passed on, having asked for the Colonel. Here we were halted; I quietly advanced and inquired of the *aide-de-camp* of General Dannenberg as to the intended attack. From him I gained the following information: A sortie on a very large scale was to take place from the Karabelnaya in order to attack the Victoria Redoubt; to this sortie we were to form the left flank and drive in the English troops to the windmill, while the troops that were in our second line were to throw up a trench along the line of heights.

For this purpose each man was to bring with him a gabion or fascine. We, having succeeded in our object, were to retire behind this trench and throw up batteries in order to drive the Allies from the position they occupied on the plateau. General Liprandi was in the mean time by means of manoeuvres on the plain to engage the attention of the troops before him, and the regiment of Minsk was to make a sortie from the bastion 5. The troops told off for the purpose of attacking the position of the Allies at Inkerman were as follows:—

The column that made the sortie from the town under General Soimonoff consisted of the following regiments:—

Of the 10th division.

1. Regiment of Ekatherinenburg 1st brigade.

2. Tomsk. . . . . .2nd brigade.
3. Kolivan . . . ." . . . "

16th division,
4. Vladimir . . . . 1st brigade.
5. Sousdal. . . . ." . . . "
6. Onglitz. 2nd brigade

17th division.
7. Bontirsk. . . . . 1st brigade.

Not more than two field batteries came out of the town with
the column of Soimonoff, as there was scarcely any field artillery
in Sevastopol. The guns belonging to this column crossed the
bridge that had been constructed during the night over the river
Chernaya at Inkerman, under the cover of the column of Pavloff, and were to have joined that of Soimonoff on the heights.

The column of General Pavloff that crossed the river Chernaya by the Inkerman Bridge consisted of the following regiments:

11th division.
8. Regiment of Selesghinsk . . . . . .1st brigade.
9. Yakoutsk . . . ." . . . "
10. Okhotsk. . . . . 2nd brigade.

17th division.
11. Borodino . . . . .2nd brigade.
12. Taroutine . . . ." . . . "

With this column there crossed as many guns as it was possible to get along the narrow causeway.

Thus, at the battle of Inkerman there were twelve regiments:
those of the 16th and 17th divisions were less than 3000 men
each, while those of the 10th and 11th were more than 3000
men, so that at a fair average they may be placed at 3000 men,
which will give 36,000 bayonets; there were not less than ten
batteries or 120 guns actually engaged, with about 3000 artillerymen, besides two batteries that remained in reserve on the
other side of the river. There were also engaged two battalions

of riflemen; so that in round numbers there were about 40,000 men engaged.

When the colonel returned from General Dannenberg he sent for the commanders of battalions, who informed us that our regiment was to cross the bridge first, and that we were to occupy the heights to the south of the bridge. The 3rd and 4th battalions were to form in front in columns of companies, while the 1st and 2nd were to form in the rear in attacking columns of battalions. Under our cover the artillery were to gain the heights by two roads; one to the left that passes above the quarry ravine, and the other to the right, which had been constructed by the 6th Sapper Battalion by order of Prince Menschikoff, and was finished in July 1854; this road was very important during the battle of Inkerman.

After a halt of about half-an-hour we began to move down the hill towards the river Chernaya. We advanced in the most perfect silence and order, though I never for a moment imagined that the Allies would allow us to reach the bridge by the long and narrow causeway that led to it, as a couple of field-pieces on the road above the bridge would have swept it from end to end. We however reached the bridge that had been hurriedly constructed during the night by sailors, in safety: we asked these men if they had seen the enemy; they said he was either asleep or making his coffee, as they had been all round the hills and seen no one. Then we all began to consider the success of our enterprise as certain, for it was evident the Allies would be surprised. Having crossed the bridge, we moved a little to the right, and then began to ascend the hill. Not a shot was heard on either side.

The day now began to break, but we were enveloped in such a thick fog that the rays of the sun could not penetrate, nor could we see far before us. I remarked that in the faces of all the men near me there was depicted a deathly paleness, and I turned to the commander of the battalion, Captain Vaksmout (who was acting in this duty, as our Major had not yet thought fit to join the regiment), with the remark, "How pale you are!"

He said, "Well, look at yourself!" and having in my pocket a small hair-brush with a looking-glass at the back, I ventured to take a peep at my own face, and found that like the rest I was as pale as a sheet.

When we were half way up the hill the colonel halted us, as our first line had reached the summit. To the right of us we could hear the artillery firing. Before daybreak the regiments of the 10th and 16th divisions had left the town and formed in front of bastion No. 1.; the regiment of Boutirsk came out of bastion No. 2. As the day broke these troops began to move. In the rear of our regiment, the regiment of Borodino had crossed the bridge and had climbed the hills more to the right of us. Immediately behind this regiment the artillery had begun to cross, and took the new road of Prince Menschikoff, in order to join the column coming out of the town. When these batteries had passed, the rest of the guns began to cross, and took the road to the left above the quarry ravine, under cover of our regiment. The 11th division, provided with gabions and fascines, was to throw up the trench behind us on the heights as we advanced.

Suddenly, without any apparent reason, our front line turned to the left, and Lieutenant-Colonel Smelkoff, commanding the 4th battalion, shouted "To the left!" We soon afterwards discovered that they had seen the regiment of Ekaterinenburg moving in that direction, and they had done the same.

The colonel inquired who had given the order to the left, since General Dannenberg had ordered him to crown the heights and wait for orders; "besides," added he, "don't you see the artillery is coming up the hill, and we are placed here to cover its advance?" But no one listened to his remonstrance, and the 3rd and 4th Battalions began to descend the hill towards the road with loud hurrahs! When the commander of our battalion asked of the colonel what we were to do, he said, "Oh, go!" with an angry wave of the hand.

We formed into columns of companies, and descended to the road, which we crossed, and reached the quarry ravine just above the quarries; the descent was excessively steep, and the men became broken; many of them left here their knapsacks, great-coats, and sapping tools. By dint of great exertions I managed to keep my company together, nor would I allow the men to abandon any of their knapsacks. The ascent from the quarry ravine was more difficult than the descent, as it was so steep that we were obliged to drag ourselves up by catching hold of the brushwood. For anyone who knows the ground I have only to say that it was just above the limekiln.

I managed, however, to keep my company together, as I knew if they once broke I could not collect them again. In the mean time the men of the 3rd and 4th battalions were standing before a small battery, shouting hurrah! And waving their caps for us to come on; the buglers continually played the advance, and several of my men broke from the ranks at a run. I still, however, kept them together. As we got higher up the hill we began to hear the whistle of the rifle-balls about us, and some of the men began to remonstrate with me that we should be too late, that the battle would be over before we could get up. I said I thought there would be plenty for us to do as well as for those behind us.

Around the battery there was a crowd of soldiers in disorder, broken by the ground they had crossed; to the right was part of the regiment of Borodino, the rest of which, like ourselves, was still advancing. The regiment of Ekaterinenburg was to the right of us, and afterwards descended into the ravine, where the soldiers helped themselves to what they liked best out of the knapsacks of our men. They then formed in a second line in the rear, and a little below the regiment of Borodino and our own. I brought my company to within forty yards of the battery, and, turning to see in what order they were, I perceived a great many people on the spur where the first lighthouse was situated; I took them for the Grand Dukes with Prince Menschikoff and their suites.

I said to the men, "Do you see there? At the lighthouse are the Grand Dukes; mind you don't disgrace yourselves in their sight!" Every man in the company turned his head, and in answer to my question, "Do you see them?"

"We do, sir!" was the answer of the whole company.

"Then forward with the bayonet!" shouted I. The crowd gave way right and left, as with a loud hurrah my company of about 120 men rushed at the battery; the men who were in disorder followed our example, and moved forwards. I scrambled up the barbette of the battery, and saw by the red coats that we were engaged with Englishmen. They had, too, tall black caps: what they were I did not know, but I have since learnt that they were the English Guards; they retired about 400 yards, and opened a fire of rifles upon us.

The battery was constructed for two guns, but they were not there; inside the battery were kettles boiling on the fires, and most probably the Guards were preparing their breakfast; several soldiers went into the battery, and began to look for plunder. Here my company became mixed up with the crowd, so that it was impossible to restore order. Close to me stood a young ensign of the name of Protopopoff, and, seeing that he looked dull, I asked what was the matter.

"Ah!" said he, "tell my uncle to write home, and say that I was killed at the battle of Inkerman!"

His uncle was in our regiment. I told him that he ought not to joke like that, "for don't you see the day is ours?"

I had hardly time to pronounce these words before he was struck in the left side by a rifle-ball, and died almost immediately. Shortly after this I received a blow on the left shoulder from a small stone, and I heard from all sides cries that "the Ekatherinenburgers are killing us!" I asked what was the matter, and at the same instant a man fell dead beside me. I ordered the men who were near me to see where he was shot. They said in the back of the head, so there could be no longer any doubt. Taking with me six men of my company, I went down to the regiment of Ekaterinenburg, which I found about half way down the hill in a disorganised mass and firing. On my asking them what they were firing at, they said they were firing over our heads.

"How can you be firing over our heads when you are killing our men?" I tried to reason with them, and persuade them if they would not advance at least to cease firing, when a man stepped out and fired close to me. I could contain myself no longer, but began to belabour him with the flat of my sword, when I saw a major coming up to me, and I rushed to meet him.

"What on earth are you about? Why don't you look to your men? Why don't you advance? If you won't advance, at least order your men to cease firing, for they are killing us!"

The major said in a plaintive voice, "What can I do when they have killed more than half of us!"

Thinking he meant the enemy, I said, "And is that a reason why you should now kill your own people?"

"No," said he, "it is they" pointing to the men, "who have shot us; I am the only field officer left, and what can I do with such ruffians!"

"It is a shame, Mr. Major," said I, "to fear your own men!"

We were joined by an officer from the regiment of Borodino, who added his remonstrances to mine, but without effect. The major left us, and went farther down the hill out of the way. I returned again to the battery, but here reigned such confusion that it was impossible to distinguish the men of my own regiment. Suddenly a cry was raised that we were being out-flanked; I shouted for the men of my company, but it was of no use, and the sergeant-major said they were mixed up with the others, so that it would be impossible to separate them.

At this time I met young Ensign Arnaoutoff, who said, as coolly as possible, "How do you do? They would not let me have my sleep out today!"

This man was always thought a coward in the regiment because he was slow! I asked some of the officers what we had better do, advance or retire, as it was useless to remain where we were; but they were all undecided, saying that the colonel was not there, nor were the commanders of battalions, and in many cases the captains had been killed. In the mean time the fire from below kept increasing, for it appeared that the Ekatherinenburgers had resolved on our destruction. (Ensign Lepinsky of our regiment had a Russian ball extracted from his heel after the battle.) I afterwards learnt that the commander of a battery on the hill had brought four guns to bear upon us, as, seeing we were fired at by a Russian regiment, he took us naturally enough for the enemy; fortunately for us an officer, who knew who we were, rode up to the guns when they were ready to fire, otherwise our loss would have been much heavier than it was. The picket that we found in the battery still remained about 400 yards from us, firing, and when in some cases I suppose they ran short of ammunition they came nearer and threw stones. The chaos was something extraordinary around the battery: some of the men were grumbling at the regiment of Ekaterinenburg, others were shouting for artillery to come up, the buglers constantly played the signal to advance, and drummers beat to the attack, but nobody thought of moving; there we stood like a flock of sheep.

It will be seen that three regiments or twelve battalions attacked a battery in which there was a picket of about forty English soldiers, and, having gained possession of the battery, no one ever thought of pushing on, nor did we know which direction to take. On the right flank and centre things were not in a much better state. At the same time that the column of Soimonoff came out of the bastion 1., the regiment of Boutirsk came out of bastion 2. One of the first shots that were fired killed General Soimonoff, which was the chief cause of the disorder in the 10th division. The regiment of Ekaterinenburg having killed the greater part of its own officers (only one-tenth of the number came out of action), the men, having no one to command them, wandered Heaven knows whither, and led our brigade astray, which brought us up to the two-gun battery, where we ought never to have been.

The regiment of Tomsk took that of Boutirsk for French, for two reasons—the first was the density of the fog, and the second because the men of the regiment of Boutirsk wore caps in shape very much like the French *kepi,* only higher.[1] The regi-

---

1. These caps were introduced by Chomoutoff, the *ataman* of all the Cossacks, under whose orders the 1st brigade of our division had been placed.

ment of Tomsk opened fire upon the regiment of Boutirsk, and then rushed in with the bayonet, only discovering their blunder when close upon them; and several officers ran towards them shouting that they were the regiment of Boutirsk. One drunken man, however, took a sergeant of the regiment of Boutirsk prisoner and brought him into the town. In vain the sergeant assured him that he was Russian like himself, advancing as a proof that he spoke his own language.

"No, no," said the hero, "that will not do. When you get into trouble you can all talk Russian! After this nothing shall persuade me that all Frenchmen don't know our language!"

The regiment of Kolivan advanced up the ravine and took prisoners an English picket. General Dannenberg, seeing that his front line was in disorder, ordered the second to advance. The three regiments of the 16th division, with two of the 10th division, advanced with the bayonet, but were beaten back.

About half-past nine we could see some troops advancing towards us, and the buglers sounded "To the left about!" All turned round and began to run helter-skelter. The officers shouted for the men to halt, but to no avail, for none of them thought of stopping, but each followed the direction his fancy or his fears prompted. I went straight down the hill towards the river. During this flight not a few were shot down, as the fire of rifles increased every minute. We met the commander of the 4th battalion, Lieutenant-Colonel Smelkoff, who was walking slowly about, holding carefully his left hand. In answer to my question what was the matter, he said he was wounded. I then asked him what he thought would come of all this disorder, as the Ekatherinenburgers had been firing into us.

He answered, "God only knows!"

In the mean time the three regiments of the 11th division crossed the bridge and gained the heights by the Menschikoff road.

Our men began to collect near the aqueduct that crosses the end of the quarry ravine; but even here the rifle-balls reached us, and the men began to run towards the bridge. Suddenly, as if he fell from heaven, appeared amongst us the general of our division, Kiriakoff, whom we had not seen for some days. "Halt, halt!" shouted he, waving franticly his Cossack whip; but the soldiers paid little attention to him, so, in order to gain proper respect from the men, he began to beat them with his whip, shouting that the officers did not attend to their duty, or the men would never have run.

Some of the men, who could not bear to see this, shouted, "Go up there yourself. He was not to be seen in the fight, but he makes himself felt now it's over." Some English soldiers, who had been made prisoners, were brought past, and I could judge by their expression of countenance that they were extremely surprised at the extraordinary conduct of our general.

The first company of carabineers, the first company of the battalion to which I belonged, came out of the quarry ravine under the arches. It was commanded by Sub-Lieutenant Ivanoff, whom I asked what had become of Captain ———, whose company it was.

"He is gone to the field-hospital," was the reply.

"Is he wounded?"

"Oh, no."

"Then how could he leave his company?"

"Very simply. With our company was Colonel Gordeieff, Captain ——— came up to me and told me to do his duty for him while he went to the field-hospital. After this he made the best of his way out of danger."

I put it to all—is it not enough to disgust one with a service in which a man, because he is the son of a major-general and the former colonel of a regiment, can with impunity desert his post in the field of battle? Not only was nothing said about a court-martial, but this man was one of the first to be rewarded for his distinguished conduct; while others, who faced all the dangers and were in the thick of the fight, were overlooked altogether. This same company of carabineers remained close to the quarries and never came near the two-gun battery.

Behind the rock to the eastward of the ravine we began to

bring into something like order our scattered forces. In this the general was very active. We then moved on and up a little hill on which there were some old barracks. We were in one mass under the command of Major Karounine, the commander of our 3rd battalion. While we halted here my servant brought me some breakfast, which proved most acceptable after our long march and fight. We then moved to the right and formed across the road, where we remained about an hour while the 11th division was engaged with the bayonet, forming, as it were, the reserve to that division, which was beaten off and retreated to-wards the town.

On learning this several of the officers and one Römer, who for political crimes had been degraded to the ranks, begged of the major to advance, but this he refused to do and restrained their ardour. About this time there came up to us Sub-Lieuten-ant Sabakine, on crutches. He had so chafed his foot during the long marches we had made on the preceding days that a large wound was formed, and when we moved in the morning he was left at the bivouac. When he heard that the regiment was gone to fight at Inkerman, he limped after us as best he could, and he only regretted that he had come too late to be of any service. This is true courage, which one involuntarily admires. We asked him if he had seen Captain ——.

"Oh, yes," said he, "I saw him standing on the other side of the bridge, smoking cigarettes d'Odessa, and who do you think is with him? ——!"

"Is he wounded?" I asked.

"No; he said he felt a little sick, and so came away."

"It is disgraceful to find officers such cowards!"

The major wanted an officer to go to the bridge to ask the colonel for orders. I offered to go, and found him near the bridge with the general, who ordered us to retreat to the river, which we did along the road.

During the retreat, or rather flight, from the two-gun battery, we lost a great many men from our ignorance of the ground; every one ran according to his own judgement, and many found themselves at the top of high precipitous rocks or the quarries, and such was the panic that had taken possession of the men that many of them, making the sign of the cross, threw themselves over and were dashed to pieces. I saw more than one instance of this; numbers, especially wounded men, crept into the caves that abound here, and were never heard of more.

When we got near the bridge we could no longer hear the sound of the whistling bullets. The colonel ordered us to muster our companies, and I found that I had only forty-five men left out of one hundred and twenty, the number with which I left the bivouac that morning. The first (carabineer) company that had been with the colonel, and under the command of Captain ———, was found to have lost only three men (!); but as it had given men to make up the other companies, it had lost twenty men altogether.

While we were here the men began to show their prizes: one had found in the battery a revolver with one charge still in the chamber, but the cap was gone—perhaps that one charge missing fire had cost the owner his life. Another man obtained and brought away an English artillery saddle, a third had a knapsack. The officers of the regiment collected round the colonel, and General Kiriakoff joined the party and told us that he had complained to the Grand Dukes that Prince Menschikoff used him very badly, since he had sent one of the brigades of his (17th) division into the town, and the other had been given over to General Dannenberg, thus depriving him altogether of his command. I thought at the time that most probably Menschikoff had understood the man, and had learnt that his conduct at the Alma did not inspire confidence.

While we were here, a *flugel aide-de-camp* rode up and asked the colonel who had ordered him to retreat. General Kiriakoff answered for him and said that a *flugel aide-de-camp* had galloped up and told them to retire. The *flugel aide-de-camp* rode off without saying a word. Will the reader compare this with what I stated above about my going for orders, when I saw no *flugel aide-de-camp*? Nor do I believe any orders had been given for us to retire. We remained near the bridge about half an hour, when we crossed it and the causeway. About twenty minutes afterwards the enemy's artillery appeared on the heights and opened fire on us, and then off we ran as fast as our legs could carry us, though the general tried to stop the men, in which we partly succeeded.

The regiments of the 11th and 16th divisions with the regiment of Boutirsk retreated into the town; the 16th division and the regiment of Boutirsk retired behind bastion 2; the 11th division with all the artillery retreated to bastion 1. Yes, all the guns, to the number of upwards of a hundred, with the exception of those that were disabled and left the field across the bridge before the battle was over, retreated into the town. The retreat of the artillery by a narrow road was attended with great difficulty, as the infantry had retired first, thus leaving the guns to shift for themselves. It was fortunate for the fate of these guns that Totleben rode out to see what was going on, and, remarking the confusion that deigned, he sent back two battalions of the regiment of Boutirsk with orders to remain till every gun had entered the town. During the battle General Dannenberg sought the posts of the greatest danger, and, seeing that he had not succeeded in his plan, he appeared to seek death.

Two horses were killed under him, and the greater part of his staff were either killed or wounded. The Grand Dukes were present at the battery near the first lighthouse with Prince Menschikoff, and from this point a courier was despatched to the Emperor announcing the successful commencement of the battle. They afterwards crossed the Inkerman Bridge while the troops were advancing, and entered the town by the Menschikoff road near the bastion 2. From this they went into the Malakhoff Bastion, where they remained about half an hour, when, seeing that their hopes of a victory were disappointed, they crossed over to the north side of the harbour.

A sortie was made from bastion 5. by the regiment of Minsk of the 14th division with one light field battery, under the command of General Timofeyeff, when it was said that they spiked fifteen guns in a French battery.

In the town there were not left more than 7000 regular troops, and these dispersed over a large space; they consisted of the following regiments, *viz.*: the regiment of Tobolsk of the 10th division, the regiment of Volhynia of the 14th division, the regiment of Moscow of the 17th division (of this regiment there were not more than 300 men left after the battle of the Alma), two battalions of Cossacks of the Black Sea, and the reserves and depots of the 13th division, that had also good cause to remember the day of the Alma. These I consider as the garrison of the town, and with the sailors and gunners would amount to about 20,000 men. Had a small force attacked boldly the town on that day, nothing could have been easier than to succeed.

The loss on the side of the Russians at the battle of Inkerman was very great, and, as far as I was able to ascertain, amounted to 12,300 rank and file, killed, wounded, and missing; our regiment alone lost 1600 men, and my company 75. The loss in officers was also very great; our regiment lost 28 out of 50; in some other regiments the proportion was greater, as, for instance, in the regiment of Ekatherinenburg. General Soimonoff was shot through the body and died shortly afterwards; two other Generals, Villebois and Okhterloné, were wounded, as well as the colonels of five regiments. General Kishinsky, the commander of the artillery, received a contusion from a splinter of a shell.

At the same time that the battle of Inkerman was being fought, General Liprandi, under the orders of Prince Gortchakoff I., manoeuvred on the plain of Balaclava, which he threatened in order to keep the attention of the column left for the defence of that place engaged.

After all was over Prince Menschikoff was entirely at a loss how to send the disastrous intelligence to the Emperor after the favourable report he had despatched in the morning. Accordingly a council of war was held that evening at which were present the Grand Dukes. At this council it was resolved that General Dannenberg should go himself to St. Petersburg and tell the Emperor what had happened. The idea was first proposed by the Grand Duke Nicholas, saying, "Your Excellency knows well the ground and your own plan of attack, so I should advise you to go yourself, and relate to my father all the particulars in order to prevent mistakes."

I think the journey to St. Petersburg must not have been very agreeable when the General reflected that at the end of it he would have to stand before Nicholas with the report of a defeated attack which he had planned,

I learnt afterwards that, at the council of war that preceded the battle of Inkerman, General Liprandi had proposed with the other two divisions of the 4th Corps (Liprandi commanded the 12th division) to attack the heights of Balaclava, which, having succeeded, would have deprived the English of the harbour, of so much importance to them; they would then have been obliged to get their supplies from Kamiesh or Kazakh, which would greatly have increased their difficulties during the winter, as the distance is much greater. It is very probable that this plan would have succeeded, as the position of Balaclava was not then fortified as it has been since. The plan of General Liprandi was not received, as he was only a general of division, and Dannenberg commanded a *corps d'armée*; the rank a man holds in Russia is generally considered a criterion for his abilities, though the rule does not always hold good. General Dannenberg, however, is a very clever general, and completed his education at the Military Academy, and, though his plan was well conceived and promised every success, yet he had not energy sufficient to carry it out in detail.

After we moved from the bridge we retired to our old position on the heights of the Belbek, which we reached about five o'clock in the evening, and immediately lay down to sleep after our hard day. The disorder that reigned in the town that night was beyond conception; all the field-guns that had been engaged at Inkerman were crowded together in the Karabelnaya, so that there was hardly room to move; they were transported across the great harbour to the north side in steamers during the latter part of the night. A field-hospital had been established beyond the Inkerman Bridge, and all night boats and small steamers were employed transporting the wounded to the barracks on the north side of the harbour. Another hospital was established in the Karabelnaya.

On the morning of the 6th, having recovered from our fatigues of the day before, we began to inquire after the fate of our fellow officers, and we learnt that one was wounded and in the hospital, another killed, and so on. Every one lost his courage when he saw the ravages that had been committed in our ranks; no laughing or jesting was heard in the regiment, but every man seemed most fervently to thank his Maker that he had been preserved through this terrible day, the like of which has never been seen, when the third of an army was destroyed in one battle. I have no doubt that some of our officers fell from the balls of their own men; I know that Captain Goreff was shot by the soldiers of his own company, and do not think that was a solitary instance.

At 11 a.m. an order came that Prince Menschikoff would inspect the troops at 1 o'clock; at half-past 12 we stood to our arms, and soon afterwards he rode up in apparently a very ill temper, as he wore a settled frown on his brows; he spoke in a very low tone of voice, and thanked us in the name of the Emperor for the gallantry we had shown in the action of yesterday. He then rode on to the regiment of Borodino, that stood next to us, when the officers of that regiment and ours stepped out of the ranks and complained that the regiment of Ekaterinenburg had fired at us; and that when we had remonstrated with the major, who was the senior officer of the regiment, and told him to order his men to cease firing, as they were killing us, he refused to interfere. As no one knew the name of the major, a captain of the regiment of Borodino offered to go with the prince to point him out; nothing was done to the regiment, and I have reason to believe the major escaped all punishment, for we never heard any more about the matter.

The next day (7th) we were told that the Grand Dukes would inspect us, and about one o'clock they came up to us, thanking us in the name of their father for the gallant manner in which we had fought; they added that they thanked us too in their own names, as our regiment was the first in the two-gun battery, and that for our gallantry they had each received the cross of St. George, which they pointed to on the breasts of their grey great-coats. I could not help reflecting that we had done little to be thanked for, save losing our men. A profound melancholy was remarkable in the expression of countenance of these two young princes; no doubt they were touched by the loss of so many human lives. The regiment of Borodino could not muster eight hundred men after the battle of Inkerman, so that, if courage is to be judged by the extent of the losses, theirs must have exceeded ours.

On the morning of the 8th I went to the barracks on the north side of the harbour to see a comrade who had been wounded on the 5th. On reaching the barracks the scene presented there was so replete with horrors that nothing will ever efface it from my memory; not only were the buildings full of miserable maimed objects, but the courtyards were crowded with dead and dying, who lay there in their agony, with their ghastly wounds unwashed and undressed, in the dirt and dust. Not only were these unfortunate men unattended to, but the dead were not carried away. I had to pass through two of these courts of suffering, which presented all the concentrated horrors of a field of battle within the smallest possible space, and without the excitement that enables one to support the sight of men in their agony after an action. I felt sick at heart, and could understand why a Russian soldier prefers death on the field to a wound, however slight.

After passing through one room full of wounded, I found Masnikoff, with whom I had sat on the same form at school, and with whom I had entered the service and the same regiment. He was wounded in the right shoulder by a rifle-ball, but no surgeon had ever examined his wound; there he lay, Heaven only knows on what, covered with blood that had flowed from his wound. He begged of me to bind him up with anything, as he could feel the ball gradually sinking inside his body; he also asked for a change of linen to be sent to him, as what he had on was saturated with blood. I asked him if a doctor had been to see him.

"No," said he, "a *feldsher*, or hospital dresser, came and dressed the wounds of those who were slightly wounded, but he said it was useless to do anything for me, as there were no hopes of my recovery, so I shall die, and I hope soon." He asked me to make such arrangements as I could about his property, and to write to his father. I asked if the Grand Dukes had been there.

"The day before yesterday they were in the next room, but they did not come in here."

In the same room with my poor comrade was an officer of the name of Ermolaëff, who had been slightly wounded with a splinter of a shell. As I knew him, I asked after his health.

"I am improving slowly," said he.

"Has your wound been dressed?" I asked.

"Yes," said he, "but I was obliged to pay those swine to get them to wash and dress my arm; the dressers won't do anything without money, —— the brutes! But I must give all praise to a poor woman from Sevastopol; she is called Maria; she attends to us as well as she can—brings us tea, washes and dresses such wounds as she is able—in fact, takes care of us all."

"Is not that the same woman," asked I, "whom I saw dressing the wounds of the soldiers in the courtyard?"

"Most probably, as no one else is likely to care for them, poor fellows!"

At this time a soldier entered the room and announced that the Grand Dukes were coming, which was a signal for all visitors to retire. I waited near the door while their Highnesses visited the wounded I had just left. Michael was the first to come out, and, as he came near me, I could remark that tears were standing in his eyes. As he passed he returned my salute, and asked whether I was wounded.

"I am not, your Imperial Highness," I answered.

"Were you in the action?"

"I was, your Imperial Highness, and have only forty-five men left in my company out of 120!"

"Yes, I remember your regiment was the first in the English battery."

"It was, your Imperial Highness."

While this conversation was going on, a number of wounded soldiers began to crawl along the ground towards us; some without arms, others without legs, each man groaning in agony; altogether there must have been near 300 of these remnants of humanity. It was a most touching spectacle. At the last question of the Grand Duke Michael his brother Nicholas came out with a stern frown on his brow. Michael made some observation to his brother in a low tone in French, and they moved away. This was a signal for the poor fellows to call the attention of their princes to them by a piteous cry of "Your Imperial Highnesses!" and all holding up to their sight the remains of their mutilated limbs.

Nicholas turned and said, in what appeared to me a stern voice, "Never mind, my father will reward you all!"

"Yes," said one, "but he cannot return me my arm!"

The Grand Dukes hurriedly passed through this crowd, in which they were aided by their *aide-de-camp*, who removed the men who lay in their path. I returned to say goodbye to my comrade and old schoolfellow, and learnt that the Grand Dukes had promised to give money to the wounded officers. From this I went into another part of the barracks to see the commander of my battalion Major Iliashenko, who was still in the hospital on account of his eyes that were injured in the town. He appeared to me to be quite well, but said he was afraid that the fresh air might prove injurious to him, though I believe he never had anything the matter with him. The Grand Dukes had asked him whether he would soon be able to join his regiment, as he appeared well. This was a good example for the young officers of the regiment!

On the 9th the celebrated Russian surgeon Pirogoff arrived at the north side. He performed a great many operations and improved the state of the hospitals. The next day he examined my comrade Masnikoff, but said he thought he was not able to bear the extraction of the ball, as it was too late; had the operation been performed earlier, his life would have been saved, He died on the 11th.

We remained on the same position till the 16th of November, and were employed making gabions and fascines, which were sent into the town. During all this time we were without any shelter, except such huts as we could erect with branches of trees, and they afforded very little protection against the weather; these huts were all blown away by the terrific hurricane of the 14th of November. After the battle of Inkerman the Grand Dukes gave to each soldier two silver *roubles*. Now only was distributed the money that the Emperor had ordered to be given to the men for the first and second days (17th and 18th of October), though it was received on the 29th of October; but as the battle of Inkerman was then foreseen, it was not considered advisable to give money to men who might be killed; it was kept till after the battle, and what ought to have belonged to the killed went into the pockets of the officers commanding regiments.

The Grand Dukes remained a week after the battle of Inkerman, visited the town, and it was said they went into the bastions. They went to the hospitals daily, though very little improvement in the attention to the wounded seemed to result from their presence.

Sick and wounded were sent daily to the hospitals at Bakchi Sarai, Simpheropol, and other places. As the means of transport were not great for this purpose, all the wagons that were returning empty were forced to carry these unfortunate men—even private wagons were seized.

Several of our officers who had the advantage of influence, finding the affairs we were likely to be engaged in not at all to their taste, sought and found staff and other employment at Simpheropol and in the interior, that took them out of danger in the event of another battle like that of Inkerman, for they did not like the idea of again meeting the English and French in the field. These men were all Russians; not a single Pole shirked a duty or refused to meet the enemy's bayonets. In Simpheropol it became very easy to obtain a certificate of a wound that incapacitated the possessor for military service; the average price was about 400 silver *roubles*; many availed themselves of this.

CHAPTER 7.

Balaclava

On the 17th of November our brigade was ordered to Chorgoun, and we marched thither on the same day. At the descent of the Mackenzie Heights we were ordered to extend our men as much as possible, so that the Allies might take us for a much larger body of troops than we really were. We reached Chorgoun about four o'clock in the afternoon. The position pointed out for our regiment was before the bridge (Traktir), on the low rising ground, where a redoubt for twelve guns was afterwards constructed. The regiment of Borodino took up a position opposite the ford.

Before our arrival at Chorgoun, the 12th division was stationed there under General Liprandi, who lived at Chorgoun. The regiments of this division occupied the same positions they had gained on the 25th of October. The Hussar brigade of the 6th Cavalry division was on the left bank of the river, opposite the regiment of Borodino, with two sotnias of Cossacks. Prince Gortchakoff I., who commanded all the troops in this position, lived at the village of Karlovka. The men of the 12th division had many hardships to support, as there was no water on the ground they occupied; consequently the kitchens were near the canal, and the food was carried to the men in casks or camp-kettles, as the soldiers were never allowed day or night to quit their arms.

From the 18th to the 27th of November we remained here.

Prince Gortchakoff I. was much occupied in fortifying the position of Chorgoun, so that the men of our brigade were employed some upon the works themselves, and others in preparing gabions and fascines. The idea of the Prince was to fortify Chorgoun and then withdraw for the winter the troops that were on the left bank of the river. He said the position of Chorgoun was of the greatest importance, since it kept the enemy from the road to Korales and Bakchi Sarai. The fortifications were as follows:—opposite the bridge, and in front of our regiment, a redoubt was constructed for twelve field-pieces; opposite the ford, near the bald hill, at the foot of the Chorgoun hills, on which was the Chorgoun telegraph, a battery for eight guns; a little above the ford, at the foot of the bald hill, another battery for eight guns, six of which would bear on the stone bridge and the other two on the river. A battery was erected in the ravine of Karlovka above the village. Besides these batteries three parallel trenches connected by zigzags were thrown up on the hill of the telegraph. Notwithstanding these labours we were obliged to do the duties of the advanced posts every third or fourth night.

General Liprandi wished to fortify the position in a very different manner. He said that the works thrown up by Gortchakoff were useless; but that good batteries ought to be erected on the hills on the left bank of the river, as on that ground a battle must be fought in the spring. Prince Gortchakoff would not consent to leave any troops on the left bank, as he said the swelling of the waters of the river in the spring would cut off their retreat, to prevent which General Liprandi said it would only be necessary to erect two bridges across the river. Gortchakoff I, and Liprandi could never agree; while the general of our division, Kiriakoff, agreed with the prince in everything, for he commanded the 6th corps, of which our division formed part.

The works of Chorgoun were indeed of little use. In the first place, the redoubt that ought to have enfiladed the bridge did not answer the purpose for which it was intended, as it was too high up the hill and consequently too far off. It was also easy to be taken in flank; and, as it was a closed work, there was not room for twelve guns with their horses and tumbrels—not to mention a battalion of infantry that ought to hold it as well as the artillerymen. The prince wanted our men to erect their huts inside this redoubt. The batteries at the ford were better, but useless, as the position might have been gained without coming under their fire. The battery behind Karlovka was the best of all, perhaps; only in an attack, if the enemy had pressed on, it would have been extremely difficult to save the guns out of it.

What the trenches were intended for no one knew, unless it was that Prince Gortchakoff thought he should frighten the Allies by his earthworks without any guns. But the chief blunder was in overlooking a hill on the left bank of the river, that completely commands the position of Chorgoun up to the foot of the Mackenzie Heights. This is the hill on which stands now the Sardinian observatory.

Five days after our arrival at Chorgoun the brigade of cavalry left during the night for Bakchi Sarai, as forage began to get very scarce; they were succeeded by the regiment of Cossacks of Zolotoroff.

The constant differing in opinion between Prince Gortchakoff and General Liprandi caused the former to represent to Prince Menschikoff that the 12th division had suffered much from its fatiguing outpost duty, and that it would be advisable to relieve it. Accordingly the order came for the 12th division to go to Inkerman, as the 16th would relieve it. This was what Prince Gortchakoff wanted, as the 16th division formed part of the 6th Corps which he commanded; consequently he would have no one to deal with but his own immediate subordinates. During the night of the 27th-28th, General Liprandi left Chorgoun and took up his position at Inkerman, near the post-house. The 16th division arrived on the 28th, and at five o'clock that afternoon Prince Gortchakoff placed his troops in the following manner:—the 2nd brigade of the 16th division occupied Hasford's Hill, where the Sardinian observatory has since been erected. Of this brigade the regiment of Kazan was on the right bank of the Soukhaya River, and that of Ouglitz on the left.

Of the 1st brigade, the regiment of Vladimir occupied our old position; while on the hill nearer to Chorgoun was the regiment of Sousdal. The regiment of Borodino of our brigade moved back behind the battery; while our regiment moved behind Chorgoun, which is in the ravine leading up to the Mackenzie Heights. With these six regiments there were only two batteries. On the other side of the river there were only Cossack pickets, with the exception of the 2nd brigade of the 16th division, that was near the river. Prince Gortchakoff I. was satisfied that he had concentrated his forces on the right bank of the river. He is reported to have said that, with these arrangements, he was not afraid of 40,000 of the enemy's troops.

From the 28th November to the 4th December we remained in these positions, engaged in completing the earthworks planned by Prince Gortchakoff. We began to think these works would be endless, and they kept the men from hutting themselves; besides no one could see the use they were likely to be. We were obliged to make a road from Chorgoun to Choulian, near which place Prince Gortchakoff constructed a battery for two guns to prevent a flank movement to cut us off through the villages of Alsu and Kutchka, but this battery was not in the right place to answer the object for which it was intended. At Chorgoun we used the English sapping-tools that had been taken by Liprandi in the Turkish redoubts, and all acknowledged their superiority over the rude Russian tools the men had hitherto used. In consequence of rains the water in the Chernaya began to rise, so as to render the communications with the 2nd brigade of the 16th division extremely difficult. Prince Gortchakoff ordered the sappers to construct foot bridges in addition to one constructed by the Tatars that already existed, but one stormy night these were all carried away. The prince was beside himself with rage at this misfortune; he determined to build a wooden bridge on piles, and for this purpose a pile-driver was brought from Simpheropol, and the timber prepared.

On the 1st of December the enemy made a reconnaissance, and the Cossack pickets retired in perfect order galloping as hard as they possibly could. All was confusion at Chorgoun, and Gortchakoff did not know what to do when the Cossacks came in and reported that the enemy was advancing with a visible and invisible force. The alarm was sounded, and we had barely time to stand to our arms before the enemy's cavalry, to the number of twelve men, were on the Hasford hill. The riflemen hurried up the hill with the regiment of Kazan, as they were at the foot near the river; but before they could get near enough, the enemy had had time to see all they wanted to ascertain; accordingly they turned round and began to descend the hill. Now was the time for the Cossacks, who had lain hidden, to gallop out of their hiding-places, and with loud shouts to follow the retreating cavalry, though they took great care not to go too near, but kept out of the reach of danger.

At this time I was standing near the Chorgoun telegraph with several other officers, who shouted: "Look, look, how our Cossacks are driving them! Our Cossacks are fine fellows!" I could not help saying, that if the commander of the party wished to get rid of the Cossacks he had only to order a halt, and to face about, and that manoeuvre would have sent all these fine fellows flying.

"Oh, no!" said they; "it would be disgraceful to run away from such a handful of men."

Prince Gortchakoff I. was much pleased when it was reported to him that the riflemen of the regiment of Kazan had driven off the enemy's cavalry, though I do not think more than three shots were fired, neither of which were effective, at least as far as I could judge. After this affair Gortchakoff only remarked the blunder he had committed in not fortifying the Hasford hill. The next day he examined the spot up to which the cavalry had come, but before that it had never entered his head that cavalry could have got up that hill. On the 3rd, notwithstanding the heavy rain, the greater part of our regiment was sent to throw up a trench and a breastwork on the summit of the hill. The superintendent of this work was the colonel of the regiment of Kazan, Colonel Hasford, and for this reason the Russians call the hill, Hasford hill.

I am much astonished that Prince Gortchakoff I. should have been entrusted with the command of a *corps d'armée*, as he had been Governor of Eastern Siberia, but had fallen under the displeasure of the Tzar, and had lost his appointment. He was a man that knew little or nothing about military matters, and yet was entrusted with the command of a *corps d'armée* before an active enemy. On the 5th of December the 16th division went into winter-quarters at the villages in the valley of Korales, on account of the extreme difficulty of getting supplies to Chorgoun. Prince Gortchakoff I. and his staff occupied the village of Orta Korales. Our brigade remained at Chorgoun with one battery of artillery under the command of the general of our division, Kiriakoff.

The reason why the 16th division was not left here, was because it was commanded by a Pole, a very active and energetic man! This is generally the case in Russia. Poles are forced to serve, but no confidence is ever placed in them; some embrace even the Greco-Russian religion that they may not lose their employments, when they have attained a certain rank in the service. For instance the colonel of the regiment of Borodino, Verevkine-Shaluta, embraced the Russian religion that he might not lose his regiment, while on the road to the Crimea.

The whole of our brigade was stationed on the right bank of the river Chernaya about the villages Chorgoun and Karlovka. The Cossacks remained on the left bank for picket duty, and they occupied the old ground of the regiment of Kazan. After the 16th division and Prince Gortchakoff had left us, we discontinued our labours at the earthworks, and began to build huts for ourselves. The general, colonel, and major of our battalion, who joined the regiment again at Chorgoun not long before this, made themselves comfortable at the village of Chorgoun, and I followed their example by taking up my quarters in a Tatar house opposite the one chosen by the General. Here I remained up to the 5th of March, 1855. Major-General Soukhonine had charge of the pickets and advanced poets.

During the time of our occupying Chorgoun we were twice disturbed by the Allies. The first time was on the 30th of December. I was only just out of bed when a man of my company came running into my room with the intelligence that the enemy was coming. The Cossacks as usual retired without loss of time, and they were not stopped till they reached Choulian. We stood to our arms, and the first battalion of the regiment of Borodino took up its position on the hill, near the telegraph, where was the General Kiriakoff. My battalion occupied the heights to the left of Chorgoun; the second battalion of our regiment occupied the hill between the two ravines that lead respectively to Mackenzie and Choulian. The third and fourth battalions of our regiment remained without any orders from the general.

The troops of the Allies moved slowly along the Woronzow road; at 9 o'clock we saw the enemy's soldiers on the Hasford hill, on which a battery of artillery was placed, while our guns in the earthwork could not be brought to bear, as the embrasures had an entirely different direction, so they were obliged to be taken out of the battery, when they fired a few rounds upon the Hasford hill, which were promptly replied to. Our wagons and transport were at once sent off to Choulian. Our battalion was ordered to advance to the summit of the hills we occupied, and thence we could see the enemy's cavalry watering their horses in the Soukhaya River, after which they moved along the Woronzow road towards the village of Varnutka while the rest remained behind the Hasford hill

After five or six rounds from two guns, they were ordered to retire and take up a position in front of the 2nd battalion. The guns that were with the 3rd and 4th battalions of the regiment of Borodino, were also ordered to retire by the road to Choulian and to halt at the hill where the roads divided. Our battalion retired, and the 1st and 2nd battalions of the regiment of Borodino occupied our place, while the 3rd and 4th battalions of our regiment took up the position near the telegraph that had previously been occupied by the 1st battalion of the regiment of Borodino. The enemy's men descended the Hasford hill as far as the huts of the Cossacks, and some of them ventured as far as the river, but these latter were fired at by the troops on the hill beyond the river. The Allies then lighted their fires, which example we followed, and after looking at each other for some hours, they retired about 5 o'clock in the evening, and we went back to our quarters.

Then I learnt that the 3rd and 4th battalions of our regiment had retreated, under the command of the Colonel, Gordeieff, to Choulian, and that the 2nd battalion of the regiment of Borodino, also under the command of the colonel of that regiment, had thought fit to do the same. The general knew nothing of this till the enemy began to retire towards their position; he was in a fearful rage, and sent his *aides-de-camp* to find them and bring back the runaways immediately—they arrived about 9 o'clock that evening. This proves the much-vaunted discipline of the Russian army: two colonels, in the presence of their general of division, think proper, without any orders, to retire from their posts with a part of their regiments when they have an enemy before them drawn up in battle array. They could have no excuse for this conduct! They preferred their own safety to the performance of their duty!

A beacon had been prepared that we were to have lighted on the approach of the enemy as a signal to the 16th division, but on this day it would not burn, though five attempts were made to fire it. The day before, having no hay for my horses, I tried to borrow some from the artillery, but they would not let me have any. The appearance of the allied troops was a signal to destroy everything likely to be useful to them in case of our retreating, so the hay of the artillery that had been refused to me was set on fire. The same evening the Tatars brought me in my supplies, and then the artillery applied to me, but, remembering their refusal of the day before, and not approving of the system of wanton destruction, I asked what had become of all their hay.

"It was burnt to prevent its falling into the hands of the English,"

"Well, since you preferred burning it to letting me have some,

I shall keep mine for my own horses, and you must do as you can."

The Russian system of destroying everything in order to prevent its falling into the hands of the enemy is very barbarous; on this occasion the men of the regiment of Borodino attempted to destroy goods belonging to private individuals, and they even went into the huts of the men of our regiment, taking thence things belonging to the soldiers.

After this affair we received orders as to the positions we were to occupy on the hills in case the enemy should show himself again. The artillery was never after this placed in the batteries constructed for it, and they were recognised as perfectly useless. General Kiriakoff reported to Prince Gortchakoff I, who forwarded the report to Prince Menschikoff, "that with his small brigade he had opposed successfully a grand attack of the allied forces, who had intended to force their way to Korales. The loss on our side was seven men wounded, and two artillery horses."

The second reconnaissance took place on the 20th of February, 1855. On awaking in the morning I heard the general shouting, and sent my orderly to know what was the matter. He returned with the information that there was an alarm. I got ready as quickly as possible, and on going out of my hut, my servant, pointing to the Hasford hill, said, "There, sir, are the English!"

The weather was dreadful; heavy snow was driving before a fierce north wind, so that it was very difficult to distinguish anything; but on the hill there was a dark mass, and as our troops could not be there, they must be the enemy. The general hurried to the telegraph, and asked of the signal-officer where the enemy's troops were; he said he supposed they were there, pointing towards Balaclava.

"No," said the general; "they have come here! Look more attentively, and see if you can make them out; there appears to be something moving on the Hasford hill!"

The officer looked attentively, and then said, "Yes, your Excellence; there are some people on the hill, and they must be

English!"

The general called for the drummer that ought to be continually at the telegraph, but he was not to be found. The general began to storm at his *aide-de-camp,* who at length found the drummer, who beat the alarm. I was able to be in my place at the first stroke of the drumstick, and the troops took up the positions previously pointed out to them. Had the enemy descended at once to the river instead of halting on the hill, we should have all been caught napping, and fallen an easy prize, as the greater part of us were in bed and asleep. The Cossacks had remarked the advance of the troops too late, and fled to the nearest places of safety—some to Alsu, others to Baidar, thus giving us no warning. The sentry at the telegraph had not observed the troops at all till the general pointed them out, and then the drummer was not to be found.

The day was miserable and intensely cold, and as the English remained on the Hasford hill, where they lighted fires, till four o'clock in the afternoon, we of course were obliged to stop out on the hills on our side. I was not at all satisfied at being obliged to leave my warm hut, and stand all day in the cold.

"What can have forced them out on such a day?" said the soldiers. "A kind master would not turn his dog out in such weather. They must be mad!" As they retreated, one man and a mule with spare ammunition were taken. About half-past four we returned to our places. This day no one ran away, as most probably everybody calculated that the English would be prudent enough not to attempt anything on such a day.

During the winter we suffered much from want of provisions, especially after our brigade was left there alone. In December there was no transport whatever of biscuit, not to mention other things, and the regiments used to go alternately twice a week to Cherkes Kerman, across the Mackenzie Heights, to fetch biscuit; this would be about ten miles each way, over a hilly road. They generally started about 3 a.m., and returned about 5 p.m. Sometimes, from the continual rains, it was impossible for the men to go, and we were frequently without bread or biscuit for one and two days together.

The troops were much reduced in strength and emaciated by these journeys. In the month of January the supply of meat was discontinued, and the men only got *casha* [1] boiled with fat pork. I remember that on Christmas Day there was no biscuit, and the commanders of battalions sent an order through the sergeant-majors to the captains of companies, for them to tell their men that, if the general of division should ask them if they had any biscuit, they were to answer "they had!" while the men were actually the second day without biscuit, In the morning I went to my company for the purpose of accompanying it to church-parade, and to congratulate the men on their holiday, when the sergeant-major gave me the order of the major.

I turned to the men and said, "You hear what the sergeant-major says; now if anyone of you dares to tell a lie, I'll punish him!"

The sergeant-major said that it was the order of the major that they were to say they had biscuit. I told him to keep silence, or he would be the first to be punished. In the mean while orders had been given in the other companies, that, if the general should ask if they had any biscuit, the men were to say they had, and any one disobeying this order was to receive forty blows with a stick.

Luckily, or unluckily, the general came up to our battalion, and asked the men if they had any biscuit. The other companies answered in a low voice "they had," while mine shouted as loud as they could, "We have none, your Excellence!"

"Which company is it that has no biscuit?" inquired the general.

I stepped forward and said "that the whole battalion was without biscuit,"

"How is it they say they have?"

So he inquired again of the men, and the whole battalion said they had none, with the exception of a very few men, who could not overcome their fears of a flogging. The general imme-

---

1. A kind of gruel.

diately sent for the colonel, commanders of battalions, and the regimental quartermaster, all of whom he reprimanded severely; but the men got no biscuit that day, and on the next only half a ration. After the general was gone, the commanders of battalions collected the sergeants-major, and asked them which company had first answered they had no biscuit; they learnt that I had promised to punish any man who dared to lie.

When the general left, I went away too, but the sergeant-major caught me before I got home, and said the major wanted to see me; so I was obliged to turn back. I found my chief standing before the piled arms, talking with the other officers. I went up to him and asked what he wanted, when he turned, boiling with rage, and asked how I had dared to disobey his orders.

"You have no power," said I, "to order either me or the men under my command to lie, neither shall they!"

"What?"

"Yes, Mr. Major, I will always support the truth, and my men in telling it!"

"You are impertinent, sir," said the major; "how dare you speak to me like that? I'll report you to the colonel; I don't want such men as you to command companies in my battalion!"

With that he turned away and left me, and I went home. While this conversation was going on, I could hear some of the men say to themselves "This is a fine fellow; he is afraid of nobody."

This was part of the Russian system; give a man nothing to eat, and then oblige him to say he is filled, under the fear of the lash. With this state of things, it is not wonderful if some of the men should reason that it is useless to shoot the enemy, as they never did us any harm, but we had better get rid of these (pointing to the officers) now we have the chance.

I wonder what became of the regimental transport all this time, as we were supposed to have 240 horses in the regiment, while I can affirm that we never saw more than thirty of them, and these were seldom employed for the transport of provisions, which were brought chiefly on the backs of the men. There was an order from Prince Menschikoff for each regiment to provide itself with packsaddles, though I never saw one used during the four months I was at Chorgoun. I was told, however, by the officer in command of the transport company, that eighty of these packsaddles were made.

"Then why don't you use them?" asked I.

"We are keeping them new and clean in case of a review," was the answer.

This is frequently the case in Russia; as, for instance, the entrenching tools of a regiment are kept for show, but not for use.

During the winter two battalions of the reserves of the 12th division were sent to reinforce our regiment; but notwithstanding these reinforcements, we had a great number of sick, from over work and want of proper nourishment. The number of sick continually increased in the regimental hospital, which the colonel had removed from Chorgoun to Choulian, whence the more serious cases were sent to Simpheropol and other places. The men who were taken ill at the regiment were obliged to walk to Choulian, a distance of about three miles, and it was only in extreme cases when a man could not keep his legs that he was sent in a rough wagon to the hospital.

This means of transport for sick is very apt to increase greatly the symptoms, from the jolting. In the Russian army there are no hospital wagons or mule litters. It is a common saying that no profit can be made out of a sick man; so long as a man is well he is worth something, but when he is sick he is useless. The Russian authorities do not take half the care of their sick and wounded that they ought to do and might do.

About the end of February the Cossacks brought information to General Kiriakoff that in the salient angle of the French trench, not far from the Woronzow road, there was only a small picket that planted its sentries very carelessly, so that one night the Cossacks had caught with a lasso and carried off a French soldier. The general accordingly arranged to attack this picket with a band of volunteers, who, to the number of one hundred from each regiment, were ordered to assemble at the redoubt at five o'clock in the evening. Those from our regiment, among whom was Römer, were under the orders of Lieutenant Shestakoff. While they were at the redoubt the general ordered vodka to be distributed to them.

This was the first and only time I ever saw the men made drunk before going into action; and if the men have been found in that state after other battles, they must have obtained the liquor themselves, for I never saw it done but on this occasion. The plan of the attack was to advance in two columns to the face of the trench and so cut off the picket in the salient angle, take as many of the men as possible, and make the best of their way back again. They crossed the stone bridge and turned to the right about midnight. The general of division, the colonels, and others, accompanied them to the Fediukhine hills. As they approached the French trench they were remarked by a sentry, who fired his firelock, and our brave volunteers hesitated, when a command was heard from some one—"To the left about!"

On this all the men began to retreat at double quick time. In vain the officers called on them to halt—it was too late. The men were making the best use of their legs to carry themselves home, while some hid behind bushes. When they turned back, a fire of musketry was opened upon them that occasioned the loss of seven men. About a quarter of an hour after the first shot was fired, rockets and carcasses were thrown from the heights of Balaclava, lighting up brilliantly the plain, but by that time the men were far on their way home. On the arrival of the gallant band of volunteers, it was discovered that two men of the regiment of Borodino had deserted. There was a lively discussion among the officers as to who had given the order "To the left about;" but they one and all denied all knowledge of the matter, and each tried to bring it home to his neighbour. The real culprit was Römer, who, seeing the state the men were in, and not wishing them to do anything that might elate the Russian army, gave the order which produced the effect above mentioned.

During the winter Prince Gortchakoff I. inspected our brigade at Chorgoun. Previously to his arrival we were ordered to say, if he should inquire whether we received biscuit regularly, that we did. But he did not even ask our battalion, but told the men that they must support cheerfully all their hardships, as they were fighting for their faith and their Emperor; and that if they were deprived of some of their little comforts it was useless to repine for them. We supposed that he had been informed in the other battalions of our want of biscuit. In January the Grand Dukes, with Prince Gortchakoff, inspected us; but they merely rode past us and back again to the north side of the harbour, without visiting the advanced posts or inquiring after the welfare of the men. During the whole winter the general of division never once crossed the river to visit the outposts, but satisfied himself with what he could learn from the telegraph station. He was too busily occupied with cards and other duties to find time for outpost amusements.

From the time that I could distinguish good from evil I had conceived a dislike for the Russian government, which grew as I grew in years. While yet a boy at college, I was first taught the difference between a Pole and a Russian, for we were not allowed to learn the dogmas of our religion in our native language, neither were they allowed to be printed or lithographed in the Russian language, but we were obliged to copy from each other the lessons of the priest. If other forms of religion are allowed to be taught in the native language, why should an exception be made for ours?

I left the corps of cadets an officer, and remained in the regiment four and a half years, during which time I saw a good portion of the Russian empire, and was able practically to judge of the evils produced by the system of government. The Russian people I like; they are in general simple, kind, and open-hearted, hospitable to a fault,—of course I speak of the Russians in their natural state, as they are to be found in the villages—but the government under which they live is detestable and detested by Russians themselves. From the beginning of the war the Russians began to complain bitterly of the Poles, saying that they were the authors of all their mishaps; particularly those officers of the staff who were Poles. If this really be the case, why do they keep us in their service? Several times I have been insulted for my nationality while with the regiment.

One Sunday evening, while at Chorgoun, several officers collected around the music, and in the course of conversation someone mentioned that the French were carrying a mine under bastion 5., and that the Russians were counter-mining. I remarked that I thought the French sappers were better than ours. Captain Lindenbaum caught this up, and said, sneeringly; "Oh, yes! Everything that we do is wrong, and all the French and English do must be right!"

Some others said, "It's no use to talk to him, you know he is a Pole!"

But I defended myself, and the dispute grew so warm that it promised anything but a peaceable termination, and for a duel in Russia a man is reduced to the ranks, and a Pole sent to Siberia. The colonel, however, joined the conversation and ordered Captain Lindenbaum to hold his tongue.

In January there was an offer from the Emperor, for those who liked it, to enter the regiment of Imperial Rifles then about being formed. Only the officers who were well acquainted with their duty would be accepted. I requested that I might be named, as I thought it would insure more rapid promotion and enable me to visit my family, whom I had not seen for some years; but the general of division would not let me go, saying, that if he allowed his best officers to leave him, what would become of the division?

Towards the end of January the list of those who had been rewarded for the battle of Inkerman was published, and my name was not in that list. I felt much hurt at this, and the next day went to the colonel to inquire why I was not thought worthy of a reward, while those who had remained with him in the ravine, and could have added who had run away, were rewarded with crosses. The colonel appeared confused, and asked if I had commanded a company at Inkerman. I stated I had; that mine was the first company in the English two-gun battery; and that I had lost seventy-five men out of it. He said he would inquire into it, and I was to call the next day.

On the following day the colonel was very kind, said he was sorry I had been omitted, that it was all the fault of Captain Lindenbaum, but that he would recommend me at once to the general. But this, though very good on his part, was not the same to me, as any of my friends reading the list, and not finding my name, would suppose naturally that I was undeserving; besides, there were few Poles in the list, for everywhere is the same distinction made. Two days after this I went with the colonel to the general, who said he was very sorry, &c, and promised to send an express to the headquarters of the corps recommending me, which he did.

My fellow-countryman Von Römer, whom I have had occasion to mention before, was degraded to the ranks for political causes; he had twice been recommended for promotion, but the Emperor Nicholas had always answered, "Let him serve as a soldier;" for in cases of men degraded, the Emperor himself always grants the first step, the others then become an affair of routine. Römer obtained the Cross of St. George for distinguished courage at the battle of Inkerman, but he was still a private soldier.

During the winter he lived with me. In our regiment there was another man, who had been degraded for embezzling government money. This man lived entirely with the men, and contracted the habits of the Russian soldier. About the end of February I saw the regimental quartermaster, who told me that ―――― had been recommended for promotion, adding that nobody will interest himself in order to obtain the promotion of Römer, because he lives and associates with officers who are Poles. "Do you know with whom he lives?" I asked.

"No," said he, "I do not."

"Then he lives with me! But what difference can it make for his promotion if he is with officers who are his countrymen? Are all Poles to be considered revolutionists, so that if a man associate with them he is not considered worthy of promotion?"

This fact completed the disgust I had long felt for the Russian service. What could they think of me, if my taking a man to live with me because I knew he wanted society could injure his future prospects? I had heard, too, from other Poles of the formation of a Polish Legion on the Danube, and resolved, come what would, to leave the Russian army, and enter this legion, with which I fondly hoped I might one day have the pleasure of entering Poland, or at least to die in the midst of my countrymen and friends in arms—a fate far preferable to the continued insults and taunts a Pole is subject to in the Russian army, while he is at the same time shedding his blood for the cause of the unholy oppressors of his country. I felt, too, great confidence that the Allied Powers would attempt something to wrest my unfortunate country from beneath the withering yoke of Russia.

I communicated my ideas and plan to Römer, recommending him to adopt them; I then learnt that he had long entertained the idea of quitting his compulsory service, but had hitherto not been able to carry it into execution.

Having made all my arrangements, I twice visited the Cossack outposts in order to ascertain the best way to carry my plan into execution. I resolved to give a farewell dinner to such officers of the regiment as I knew best. I invited all the commanders of battalions and others of the regiment. Some of them asked me why I gave this dinner, and why I called it a farewell dinner; I said that "Life was at all times uncertain, and in the field before the enemy still more so; so that Heaven knew what might happen, and I felt convinced that I should not be long with them!"

The true meaning of this, of course nobody understood. During the dinner, all were very merry, and a better fellow than I was could not be found in the regiment or in any other; though I suspect they changed their opinion of me a few days later. After dinner I bade each one of my guests farewell, saying that we might never all meet again, but none of them took any notice of my words except to reassure me, thinking I had some presentiment of death.

On Monday, March 5th, all my arrangements were complete.

In the morning I had out my company to drill, when the commander of the battalion, who was present, thanked me for the state of efficiency to which I had brought my men. After the drill was over I thanked the men, told them they must always be obedient, and, above all things, stand up for the truth.[2] When I got home, I put together some of my linen and things I might want, giving a roll of papers, consisting of plans of the Russian positions, &c, to Römer. These plans I had shown only two days before to the officers who had dined with me.

At this time a battery of the 10th Artillery brigade was stationed at Chorgoun, and in this battery were several of my old schoolfellows, so the better to conceal my plans I invited four of them, all Russians, to take an early dinner with me, and then to ride to the outposts to see the enemy's position, as they had only just arrived in the Crimea. After dinner, having previously hired two horses from the Cossacks, at a silver *rouble* each, for a ride to the outposts, I armed myself with a pistol and sword, and gave another pistol to Römer, who accompanied me as an orderly. This I did in case we should be stopped, as we were both determined not to fall alive into the hands of the Russians. The other four officers, seeing us arm, asked if they had better not take their swords, but I said they would only be in the way and useless, since two of the party were armed; but, I added, "You can do as you like."

They were prudent enough not to take their swords, at which I was very glad; for had they had an idea of what was going on they might have opposed us, and I should have been sorry to harm them. As we were leaving Chorgoun, Captain Vaksmout met us and asked where we were going. I answered jestingly, but more in earnest than he thought, that we were going to Balaclava for coffee after dinner. We directed our course first of all to Kamara, and from that village along the outlying Cossack pickets. I was fortunate enough not to find a single officer at any of them, and the Cossacks seeing me with such a

---

2. It is a very common thing, in fact a part of the discipline, for the officers to ask questions and talk to the men in the Russian army.

suite dared not stop me, as they thought I must be some distinguished personage. As I rode along the outposts the Cossacks reported to me that all was well, and that nothing had been observed on the side of the enemy. When I had reached the last pair of Cossack sentries, I inquired if there was anybody else in front; they said there were some Cossacks there feeding their horses. "Then we'll go a little farther;" and with that we all crossed the line of outposts.

I made for a hill on which I had observed two cavalry sentries with shining helmets on their heads, which I knew could not be Russian. Römer whispered to me these men must be English or French. I said, "Don't hurry; go slowly and we are safe."

After we had crossed the Woronzow road and drew near the hill, I turned to the four artillery officers and told them if they would wait I would go on a little and ascertain whether the picket before us was Russian or not. To this they all agreed. So, taking Homer with me as an orderly, I pushed on towards the hill. The two cavalry soldiers who were on the top mounted their horses and rode down on the other side.

Römer said, "There can be now no doubt that they are English or French; let's push on."

I told him, however, not to hurry, as we could trot in; but he put his horse to a gallop, drew his pistol, looked twice behind him, and rode into the picket. I rode quietly up the hill, and on reaching the summit saw at my feet the whole plain of Balaclava, on which were a great many people hurrying hither and thither. At the foot of the hill were drawn up in two lines eight cavalry soldiers with an officer on the left flank. I saw Römer riding in and waving his cap for them not to fire upon him. I rode down the hill, past the front of the men, and halted by the side of the officer with my hand at the salute waiting for his orders. The picket was evidently taken by surprise, and did not exactly know whether they should take us for friend or foe. They began to unsling their carbines, by which arm I took them for dragoons.

Römer, in the mean while, had got into conversation, in French, with the officer in command, and explained to him the object of our arrival, &c. While we were standing here one of the four officers that had accompanied us rode up to the top of the hill to see where we were; but when he saw us in the midst of an enemy's picket, he turned back rather faster than he had advanced. Römer begged of the officer not to allow his men to fire at the others, as they had no idea where they were. I took off my cap to the one that came up the hill, and wished him good-bye. When they found we were fairly gone, they set off as hard as they could gallop, not exactly knowing which direction to take. They were all caught by the Cossacks, who, guessing what was going on, started in chase, but it was too late. A few minutes afterwards an officer arrived from Balaclava, to whom Römer explained the object of our arrival; and he turned to me with congratulations that we were in the hands of Englishmen.

We were invited to accompany this officer to Balaclava; and, as I could not talk French, I rode on in front, while Römer talked with the officer. I think I never in my life felt happier than at that moment. I felt that I had cast off the yoke of tyranny, and had hopes of knowing more of freedom than the word. The very air seemed to me sweeter than it was half a mile behind us. As we approached Balaclava a continually increasing crowd surrounded us, but the faces of all we saw were fresh and cheerful, and I remarked to my comrade that it was evident we were out of the domains of the Russian knout.

We were taken to General Sir Colin Campbell, who received us most kindly and offered us luncheon, but we said we had just dined. From Balaclava we, accompanied by an officer, went to the head-quarters of the British army. Thus, at half-past one p.m. on the 5th of March, 1855, I commanded a company of Russian soldiers, and at five p.m. on the same day I was, of my own free-will, at the British head-quarters, where I have remained up to the end of the war.

LEONAUR

ALSO FROM LEONAUR
AVAILABLE IN SOFTCOVER OR HARDCOVER WITH DUST JACKET

WELLINGTON AND THE PYRENEES CAMPAIGN VOLUME I: FROM VITORIA TO THE BIDASSOA *by F. C. Beatson*—The final phase of the campaign in the Iberian Peninsula.

WELLINGTON AND THE INVASION OF FRANCE VOLUME II: THE BIDASSOA TO THE BATTLE OF THE NIVELLE *by F. C. Beatson*—The second of Beatson's series on the fall of Revolutionary France published by Leonaur, the reader is once again taken into the centre of Wellington's strategic and tactical genius.

WELLINGTON AND THE FALL OF FRANCE VOLUME III: THE GAVES AND THE BATTLE OF ORTHEZ *by F. C. Beatson*—This final chapter of F. C. Beatson's brilliant trilogy shows the 'captain of the age' at his most inspired and makes all three books essential additions to any Peninsular War library.

NAVAL BATTLES OF THE NAPOLEONIC WARS *by W. H. Fitchett*—Cape St. Vincent, the Nile, Cadiz, Copenhagen, Trafalgar & Others

SERGEANT GUILLEMARD: THE MAN WHO SHOT NELSON? *by Robert Guillemard*—A Soldier of the Infantry of the French Army of Napoleon on Campaign Throughout Europe

WITH THE GUARDS ACROSS THE PYRENEES *by Robert Batty*—The Experiences of a British Officer of Wellington's Army During the Battles for the Fall of Napoleonic France, 1813.

A STAFF OFFICER IN THE PENINSULA *by E. W. Buckham*—An Officer of the British Staff Corps Cavalry During the Peninsula Campaign of the Napoleonic Wars

THE LEIPZIG CAMPAIGN: 1813—NAPOLEON AND THE "BATTLE OF THE NATIONS" *by F. N. Maude*—Colonel Maude's analysis of Napoleon's campaign of 1813.

BUGEAUD: A PACK WITH A BATON by *Thomas Robert Bugeaud*—The Early Campaigns of a Soldier of Napoleon's Army Who Would Become a Marshal of France.

TWO LEONAUR ORIGINALS

SERGEANT NICOL by *Daniel Nicol*—The Experiences of a Gordon Highlander During the Napoleonic Wars in Egypt, the Peninsula and France.

WATERLOO RECOLLECTIONS by *Frederick Llewellyn*—Rare First Hand Accounts, Letters, Reports and Retellings from the Campaign of 1815.

www.ingramcontent.com/pod-product-compliance
Lightning Source LLC
Chambersburg PA
CBHW021109090426

42738CB00006B/568